Geoff Lindsey

English After RP

Standard British Pronunciation Today

Foreword by J. C. Wells

Geoff Lindsey
Linguistics
University College London
London, UK

ISBN 978-3-030-04356-8   ISBN 978-3-030-04357-5   (eBook)
https://doi.org/10.1007/978-3-030-04357-5

Library of Congress Control Number: 2018964109

Cover Design: Fatima Jamadar

This Palgrave Macmillan imprint is published by the registered company Springer Nature Switzerland AG
The registered company address is: Gewerbestrasse 11, 6330 Cham, Switzerland

Foreword

The existing descriptions of standard British English pronunciation, known as RP, are outdated. People who speak like me now sound old-fashioned. This book brings things up to date. It describes the various changes that have taken place since about 1950 in the kind of pronunciation usually taught to British-oriented learners and teachers of English as a foreign, second, or additional language. It presents them in a concise, readable and teachable framework.

It will be invaluable not only to teachers of EFL, but also to everyone teaching or studying linguistics and phonetics, speech and drama, and speech and language therapy.

I first met Geoff Lindsey when he was a university student reading linguistics and phonetics. He was one of the best undergraduates I taught in my forty-plus years of university teaching. This is a book I wish I had written myself – but I don't think I would have been able to make such a good job of it as he has.

UCL   J. C. Wells
London, UK
20 August 2018

Preface

The purpose of this short book is to gather in one convenient place a description of notable ways in which contemporary standard British speech differs from the British upper class accent of the last century, Received Pronunciation (RP).

The kinds of speakers who constitute today's pronunciation models are different in social terms from the typical speakers of RP, and the sound of their speech is different, too. But around the world, knowledge of British pronunciation is still rooted in RP: wherever I travel, I find that much of what is taught about British pronunciation is out of date. The social prestige which RP once enjoyed, and the scholarly prestige of the classic works describing it, have left a legacy of conservatism.

Many people are aware that things have changed, and a number of them have asked me to write a guide to modern developments. Although information about contemporary pronunciation can be found inside several detailed books (e.g. Cruttenden 2014; Carley et al. 2017), the intention here is pick out just features that have changed, as concisely as possible.

Most publications still use the set of phonetic symbols that were chosen for RP over half a century ago by A. C. Gimson, even though by Gimson's own criteria a number of them are no longer appropriate. Gimson wrote in 1981, 'it would clearly be absurd to teach a pronunciation regarded by native speakers as old-fashioned or even comic'. But if his vowel symbols are interpreted literally, the result is an old upper-class accent which British people now find amusing. I'm sometimes told by non-native users of English that their native speaker friends find their pronunciation old-fashioned: generally speaking, this is because they were taught RP.

In my experience, users are more likely to take symbols at face value than to check the details behind them. But the established symbols must now be seen as more abstract, and treated with greater caution – especially as it's not realistic to expect EFL publishers to overhaul their symbols overnight. This book attempts to clarify differences between the symbols and reality.

In addition to changes in sounds, there are changes in sound distribution: the replacement in certain words of one phoneme with another. Distributional changes mean that some sounds are less common than they used to be, like the vowel /ʊə/ and the consonant cluster /tj/. Other sounds are more common than they used to be, such as the LOT vowel and the affricate /tʃ/. Such changes are treated in turn throughout the book, as are developments in stress, connected speech and intonation. Although a wide variety of features are covered, the book makes no claim to be exhaustive.

The book ends with a Mini Dictionary, which covers the various changes discussed from the perspective of representative words, most of them very common. The notes in the Mini Dictionary indicate which features are now firmly established as the preferred pronunciation of a word, and which are used by some but not all speakers.

To begin with, an account is given of what RP was: how it arose, what it signified, why it declined, and why, in the terms of its classical definition, it no longer really exists.

London, UK   Geoff Lindsey

Symbols and Resources

In this book, phonemic transcriptions of words in their RP pronunciations are given in slash brackets. They usually follow those given in the 14th edition of the *English Pronouncing Dictionary* (1977), revised by A. C. Gimson.

Newer pronunciations of words are transcribed both with slash-bracketed traditional symbols (where possible), and also with more modern symbols in boldface. For example:

tourist	RP /ˈtʊərɪst/	newer /ˈtɔːrɪst/ **ˈtɔːrɪst**
dissect	RP /dɪˈsekt/	newer /daɪˈsekt/ **daɪˈsɛkt**
various	RP /ˈveərɪəs/	newer **ˈvɛːrɪjəs**

Use is also made of square brackets, either to show the changing realization of individual sounds, e.g. [ɛə] changing to [ɛː], [ɒ] changing to [ɔ], or to show sub-phonemic details like dark /l/ and affrication: [ɫ], [tˢ], etc.

The book often refers to vowels by means of capitalized keywords such as FLEECE, KIT and SQUARE. Each keyword refers to the vowel contained in it. Thus FLEECE (or 'the FLEECE vowel') refers to the vowel in the word *fleece*, and also in *see, reach, piece*, etc. KIT refers to the vowel in *kit*, and also in *thing, gym,* and both syllables of *English*. SQUARE refers to the vowel in *square, chair,* and *their*; and so forth. The keywords used in this book are the ones in widespread use which were chosen by John Wells.

A chart laying out standard British vowels, with both modern and traditional symbols, can be found at the end of the book. Another resource which allows the comparison of modern and traditional transcriptions is the online searchable dictionary CUBE (CUrrent British English), at www.cubedictionary.org, edited by myself and Péter Szigetvári. There's a video which introduces the dictionary's many search capabilities.

Each word in the CUBE dictionary is linked to the site YouGlish, www.youglish.com. This gives examples of each word spoken in YouTube clips, categorized into British, American and Australian English.

Acknowledgements

The writing of this book was occasioned by my visit to Argentina, August–October 2017, and I'm grateful to Universidad Nacional de La Plata and the many other institutions which invited me; for supporting the trip, I'm grateful to Pablo Demarchi and to CPD in the Division of Psychology and Language Sciences, University College London. Thanks are due to Luke Nicholson for valuable input on an earlier draft of the book. And I happily acknowledge the encouragement and inspiration I've received across the years from my great teachers and predecessors as Director of the UCL Summer Course in English Phonetics: Michael Ashby, John Wells and the late A. C. Gimson.

The intonation figures in Chaps. 28, 29, 30 and 31 were prepared by Alejandro Arrojo.

Contents

Introduction.   What Was RP?   1

Part I   Changes: General Observations   7

Chapter 1.   The Power of Writing   9

Chapter 2.   The Special Relationship   11

Chapter 3.   Getting Stronger   13

Part II   Vowels   15

Chapter 4.   The Anti-clockwise Vowel Shift   17

Chapter 5.   FLEECE, GOOSE and Other Diphthongs   23

Chapter 6.   GOAT, GOOSE and FOOT Backing   27

Chapter 7.   A LOT More Common   29

Chapter 8.   KIT: Still Going Strong (but happY Never Existed)   31

Chapter 9.   FOOT: Even Rarer, but Still Common   35

Chapter 10.   Weak Vowel Merger   39

Chapter 11.   Two Kinds of BATH   41

Chapter 12.   PRICE and MOUTH   45

Chapter 13.   The Decline of the Centring Diphthongs   47

Part III   Consonants   53

Chapter 14.   More Aspiration (and Affrication)   55

Chapter 15.   /tʃ/ and /dʒ/: A New *si-chew-ation*   59

Chapter 16.   /tʃ/ and /dʒ/: A New *chrend*   61

Chapter 17.   Epen-t-thesis   63

Chapter 18.   Syllabic Consonants: A *little* Less *certain*   65

Chapter 19.   Glottal Stops, Part 1   67

Chapter 20.   Is /l/ Following /r/?   71

Chapter 21. G-dropping and H-dropping   73

Chapter 22. Fings to Come?   75

Part IV   Stress   77

Chapter 23. The Love of Alternating Stress   79

Chapter 24. Westward Toward America?   83

Part V   Connected Speech   85

Chapter 25. Linking /r/   87

Chapter 26. Glottal Stops, Part 2   91

Chapter 27. Vocal Fry   95

Part VI   Intonation   97

Chapter 28. Falls   99

Chapter 29. Yes-No Questions   103

Chapter 30. Continuation Patterns   105

Chapter 31. Uptalk   107

Mini Dictionary   109

Vowel Chart   146

References   147

Index   149

Introduction

What Was RP?

The Rise of RP

Around the beginning of the nineteenth century, something remarkable happened in Great Britain. All over the country, people at the top of society began to change the way they spoke: they began to adopt the speech patterns of the upper classes in the London area.

Before this, there had been greater diversity of speech among Britain's social elite. But the London area model steadily became established as uniquely respectable, or 'received'. By 1869, the phonetician Alexander Ellis could write of 'a received pronunciation all over the country, not widely different in any particular locality, and admitting of a certain degree of variety. It may be especially considered as the educated pronunciation of the metropolis, of the court, the pulpit, and the bar.'

This Received Pronunciation (RP) included fashions that had only recently arisen in the South. The word *after*, for example, was pronounced with a new broad *a* (see Chap. 11), and without its final *r* (Chaps. 20 and 25). In America, which had been settled earlier, the traditional unbroadened *a* and final *r* were preserved.

Why and how did upper class people all over Britain 'clone' the speech of the social elite in and around the capital?

© The Author(s) 2019
G. Lindsey, *English After RP*, https://doi.org/10.1007/978-3-030-04357-5_1

The answers are related to the vast empire which Britain built up in the wake of its industrial revolution. With the loss of the American colonies and the defeat of Napoleon, Britain threw its energies into colonizing Africa and Asia. For a century and a half, Britain ruled over an enormous part of the world's territory and population, its economic domination extending ever further, over countries such as China and Argentina. This era was also the era of RP.

A small country like Britain could only control a planetary empire through a strict hierarchy of power and authority. The Crown and the London court naturally sat at the top, and colonial subjects were at the bottom. Stratification and rank were vital, and this included ways of speaking. In addition, Britain's industrial powerhouse, fed by materials from the colonies, was generating a new class of people with wealth. It was important for the ambitious and aspirational to acquire the manners of those at the top, and therefore to conceal regional and social markers.

Schooling was a key element in the maintenance of both the empire and RP. The empire required a large proportion of Britain's ruling class to live abroad; they left their sons in boarding schools (known misleadingly as 'public schools') where they were conditioned to behave with the manners of those in authority, and in terms of speech this meant RP. 'Public School Pronunciation' was the name proposed for RP by Daniel Jones, the founding Professor of Phonetics at University College London.

Of course, the great majority of Britons never spoke RP, and in an age before radio many of them hardly even heard it. It was necessary to produce guides to this scarce but important commodity. Jones was pre-eminent among describers of RP, producing *An English Pronouncing Dictionary* (1917) and *An Outline of English Phonetics* (1918). Jones was also a real-life model for 'Professor Higgins' in George Bernard Shaw's play *Pygmalion* (1913), on which the musical *My Fair Lady* was later based. The play mocks the injustice of a society which condemns an intelligent woman to the gutter unless she can conceal her origins with RP, a commodity she can't afford. (Higgins teaches her as a bet.)

Things were very different in the United States. There, geographical and social origins mattered less, and the newly wealthy felt no need to ape aristocratic manners. Immigrants could emulate the speech of the ordinary Americans they mingled with, something that in Britain would have had socially restrictive consequences. Americans never had quite the same need that was felt in Britain for manuals and dictionaries showing the 'received' way to speak. And in time, America naturally came to adopt as its standard the pronunciation of the majority, a family of closely-related accents known as General American.

The Fall of RP

The twentieth century brought mass communication and culture. At first, this acted in RP's favour. RP dominated BBC radio for fifty years. 'It was no accident that RP became synonymous between the wars with the term "BBC English", for the BBC consciously adopted this type of pronunciation' (Gimson 1981). The general population were now exposed to RP regularly, and free of charge. Many people modified their speech towards it. To some it seemed that regional and social accents might be lost in RP's steady spread. Instead, the social foundations on which RP stood collapsed.

Victorian notions of social hierarchy faded as the new century progressed. Women won the right to vote and men returning from two world wars demanded greater economic equality, while colonial peoples were deemed worthy of self-government.

The pace of social change accelerated rapidly in the 1960s. Pop culture brought new glamour to Britons from the lower classes, like the Beatles. The once accepted 'superiority' of the upper classes was undermined by political scandals and a new freedom in the media to criticize and satirize. Social privilege was no longer seen as prestigious, but rather as unfair. And, for the first time, the speech patterns of those at the top began to be perceived negatively.

Increasingly, noticeably upper class speech became an object of mockery or resentment, appropriate for snobbish villains on stage and screen. Sociolinguist Peter Trudgill has written (2000), 'RP speakers are perceived, as soon as they start speaking, as haughty and unfriendly by non-RP speakers unless and until they are able to demonstrate the contrary.'

At the same time, it became easier for less privileged people to reach higher levels of attainment and success; all five Prime Ministers from

1964 to 1997 were educated at state schools. Those who rose socially felt less pressure than before to modify their speech, including those in broadcasting. And many of those at the very top, consciously or otherwise, modified their speech towards that of the middle or lower classes.

The stigmatization of noticeably upper class speech, together with the growing numbers of people from ordinary backgrounds in positions of influence, meant that it became ever less possible to talk of a 'received' accent defined by reference to the social elite.

Daniel Jones, the first UCL Professor of Phonetics, referred to RP in 1918 as the pronunciation 'of Southern Englishmen who have been educated at the great public boarding schools'. John Wells, the last UCL Professor of Phonetics, referred to it in 1982 as typically spoken by 'families whose menfolk were or are pupils at one of the "public schools"'. This conception, established in the nineteenth century, meaningful to Jones during the First World War and to Wells in the era of Margaret Thatcher, has in the subsequent decades become part of history.

In contemporary Britain, diversity is celebrated. Prominent figures in business, politics, academia and the media exhibit a range of accents. But London and the South are still dominant in wealth, power and influence. Accents of the South, particularly middle and upper-middle class accents, are heard more often than others in public life, and in the TV programmes and films that are seen internationally. Southern speech of this type is a natural teaching standard for 'British English' today; the abbreviation SSB is used for this Standard Southern British pronunciation. Some call it 'General British', but it's socially and regionally far less general than General American is in North America. It's an accent of England, and certainly not representative of Scotland, Ireland, or the former British colonies, where pronunciation is substantially different.

Although the pace of socio-phonetic change has been rapid in recent decades, there was no overnight revolution in speech patterns; modern pronunciation has much in common with RP. Indeed, some phoneticians have made efforts to keep the term 'RP' for the modern standard, by redefining it. But the term is linked in many people's minds with the past and with the upper classes. Nowadays journalists and actors will often refer to RP with precisely these connotations in mind.

A line was finally drawn under the British Empire over twenty years ago, with the handover of Hong Kong in 1997. The turn of the twenty-first century might be taken as a convenient point from which RP can be referred to in the past tense.

Part I

Changes: General Observations

Chapter 1

The Power of Writing

In Brief Numerous words now have pronunciations which are closer to the spelling than the RP pronunciations.

During the nineteenth century, literacy in Britain rose from around 50% of the population to nearly 100%. Reading became increasingly popular among the general public. There was therefore an increasing familiarity with words in their written forms – which, in English, are often quite different from their pronunciations.

As many people believed written forms to have greater authority than spoken forms, many pronunciations which had drifted away from their spelling over the years were brought back into line with it by writing-conscious speakers. The more educated may often have considered popular 'spelling pronunciations' to be mistakes. But, especially as society became more democratic, the majority pronunciation tended to become accepted as standard.

Numerous instances date from the RP era, such as the shift of *towards* from one-syllable /tɔːdz/ to two-syllable /təˈwɔːdz/. The process has continued to the present day: the Mini Dictionary at the end of this book contains a number of words which in RP had pronunciations

© The Author(s) 2019
G. Lindsey, *English After RP*, https://doi.org/10.1007/978-3-030-04357-5_2

relatively distant from their written forms, but which have been shifted closer towards the spelling. Examples:

ate
handkerchief
hurricane
interest
mayor
mosquito
nephew
often
portrait

In writing, compound words generally preserve the written forms of their component parts, even though the pronunciation may not be the same. For example, *man* is pronounced /mən/ in *postman*. Awareness of written forms may promote a feeling that such forms should be pronounced in the 'original' way: some compounds have changed since RP to make one of the components more like its independent pronunciation. Examples are *bedroom, newspaper,* and *Monday* and the other days of the week, which exhibit shifts to match the independent words *room, news* and *day.*

Not all changes have been in the direction of the spelling, however: some words, such *February* and *library,* have shifted away from their written forms (see the Mini Dictionary).

A word may be pulled in conflicting directions. The first vowel of *dissect* has shifted from the KIT vowel to the PRICE vowel under the influence of other words beginning *di-,* such as *dichotomy* and *digress,* despite the fact that the written double *ss* generally requires a preceding KIT vowel, as in *dissertation.*

Chapter 2

The Special Relationship

In Brief Many, though not all, of the contemporary pronunciation features described in this book make British pronunciation more similar to American pronunciation.

America exerts powerful cultural influence on the rest of the world. Within the English-speaking world, this includes aspects of pronunciation. Although direct cause and effect are hard to establish, many of the changes described in this book bring the pronunciations of most or many British speakers closer to those of American speakers.

Such changes include weak vowel merger (Chap. 10), yod coalescence in unstressed syllables (Chap. 15), the strengthening of some endings (Chap. 23), leftward stress shifts (Chap. 24), voicing of the fricative in words ending *-rsion*, and the pronunciation of some individual words like *ate, debris, exit, gotten, harass* and *mayor* (see the Mini Dictionary). Some recent phonetic developments are ones that are more established in America, like Uptalk (Chap. 31) and vocal fry (Chap. 27).

Nonetheless, SSB still retains its chief non-American characteristics, such as a distinct LOT vowel (Chap. 7), relatively little /t/-voicing (Chap. 19), and non-rhoticity (Chaps. 20 and 25). And some words have tended to become **less** like the American pronunciation than they were in RP,

© The Author(s) 2019
G. Lindsey, *English After RP*, https://doi.org/10.1007/978-3-030-04357-5_3

such as *contribute, controversy* and *garage* (see the Mini Dictionary). The Southern British enthusiasm for the Fall-Rise tone has probably increased (Chaps. 29 and 30). And the new popularity of TH-fronting in Britain (Chap. 22) is not matched in America.

Probably the greatest area of American influence is one that receives little attention in this book: the use of words, phrases and idioms. Many British speakers today make frequent use of words that not long ago seemed distinctively American, like *awesome, cool* (meaning 'good'), and *movie*. Idioms often become fashionable first in the US and then catch on in Britain. A few examples would be *get your act together, it's not rocket science, do the math, dumbing down.*

Britain has quite recently followed America in using the word *multiple* very often where *numerous* or *many* would previously have been more common. The same applies to the word *so* used at the beginning of an answer to a question, where *well* was previously more common.

Lastly, an Americanization in grammar has recently become evident in Britain. This is the ability to use the plain past tense where previously the *have* perfective was required, e.g. *I just ate* rather than *I've just eaten*.

Chapter 3

Getting Stronger

In Brief A number of pronunciation changes since RP can be seen as strengthenings.

English is well known for its weak and reduced sounds, e.g. the weak vowel schwa /ə/ and weak forms of functions words. RP used an especially large amount of weak and reduced sounds. In various ways, contemporary SSB pronunciations are stronger:

- Numerous individual words are now pronounced more strongly than in RP. Most of these bring the pronunciation closer to the spelling (see Chap. 1). Examples include *forehead, handkerchief, often*.
- RP allowed the lax vowels /ɪ/ and /ʊ/ to occur in many words where their pronunciation is now tense (see Chaps. 8 and 9), e.g. *happy, thank you*.
- In RP, syllables in many words were reduced to syllabic consonants, e.g. *little, certain*. Today such syllables are commonly pronounced more fully (see Chap. 18).
- RP generally had weaker aspiration of /p/, /t/, /k/ than in contemporary speech (see Chap. 14).

© The Author(s) 2019
G. Lindsey, *English After RP*, https://doi.org/10.1007/978-3-030-04357-5_4

- Final /p/, /t/, /k/ are now fairly often pronounced as ejectives [p'], [t'], [k'] (see Chap. 14). This strengthening was not characteristic of RP.
- RP was more tolerant of words with sequences of weak syllables, e.g. *primarily* /ˈpraɪmərəlɪ/. Contemporary speakers often shift the stress, lowering the number of successive weak syllables, e.g. *primarily* /praɪˈmerəliː/ **prɑjˈmɛrəlɪj** (see Chap. 23).
- The insertion of glottal stops before initial vowels ('hard attack') seems to be more common now than it was in RP (see Chap. 26).
- In intonation, RP probably made greater use of low pitch, where modern speech probably makes greater use of high pitch, including the Fall-Rise on yes-no questions and the high rise on statements (see Chaps. 28, 29, 30 and 31).

It would be wrong to say that every change since RP has been a strengthening. Nonetheless, taking all the features above into account, it's probably true to say that RP had a somewhat more lax and smooth manner of production than contemporary speech.

Part II

Vowels

Chapter 4

The Anti-clockwise Vowel Shift

In Brief Over recent decades, the qualities of most vowels have shifted in standard British pronunciation. The various changes add up to a large-scale 'anti- clockwise' shift in the vowel system. However, the phonetic symbols most widely in use for British English reflect hardly any of these changes.

The most widely used vowel symbols for British English are those pro-posed in 1962 for the upper class Received Pronunciation of the time by A. C. Gimson, then Professor of Phonetics at University College London. Gimson described his system as 'explicit on the phonetic level', meaning that he chose symbols from the International Phonetic Alphabet which best reflected RP vowels then.

Over the decades since, there have been great social and phonetic changes (see Introduction). Today's SSB, heard in television news and from many actors and politicians, is a more middle-class accent, and its vowels are substantially different.

Though the number of vowel contrasts is much the same, the qualities of most of the vowels have shifted. Some vowels are lower, some more back, some are raised, and some are more central. Together, these changes

© The Author(s) 2019
G. Lindsey, *English After RP*, https://doi.org/10.1007/978-3-030-04357-5_5

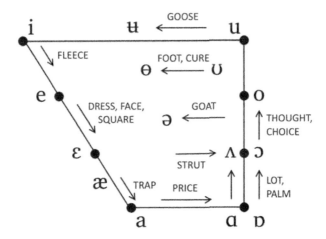

Fig. 4.1 Vowel quality shifts which have taken place in standard British pronunciation, shown on a vowel Quadrilateral with front vowels to the left and close vowels at the top. Each capitalized word represents the vowel it contains: the vowel in TRAP, for example, has lowered from [æ] to [a]

add up to a large-scale 'anti-clockwise' shift in the vowel system, which can be seen in Fig. 4.1.

The chart incorporates one change which was sufficiently advanced in 1962 for Gimson to include it in his system: this was the shift of the vowel of GOAT from [oʊ] to [əʊ]. He later wrote (1981), 'it is possible to suggest certain gross changes of quality by substituting one existing symbol for another... I indicated the shift, within the last century, of the quality of the diphthong in *go* by replacing the traditional "o" symbol for the first element by "ə", thus denoting a process of centralization.' A glance at Fig. 4.1 shows that most of the standard British vowels have by now undergone a shift of an equally 'gross' nature. For example, the GOOSE and FOOT vowels have now centralized just as the GOAT vowel centralized. Applying Gimson's own standards, then, a large-scale revision of the transcription system for standard British English vowels is due.

However, Gimson's set of symbols became 'fossilized' in British publishing around the time of his death in 1985. The result is that today's most familiar symbols give the impression that hardly anything has changed since 1962, which is very far from the truth. Those using the familiar symbols in their teaching should do so with caution and in awareness of their inaccuracies.

There have also been changes to the distribution of vowels among the words of the language, so that in many words a vowel has shifted from one member of the system to another. For many or most speakers, the last vowel of the adjective *separate* has switched from KIT to schwa; the vowel of *salt* has switched from THOUGHT to LOT; the first vowel of *tourist* has switched from CURE to THOUGHT; and so on. Such distributional changes are discussed in later chapters. But here we focus on the anti-clockwise shifts in vowel quality.

Lowered Vowels

The front vowels are lower today than in RP. The vowel of DRESS is [ɛ] rather than [e], and the vowel of TRAP is [a] rather than [æ]. However, learners of English should be aware that the [a] of contemporary TRAP is still usually more front than the *a* of most languages, including Spanish and Japanese.

In 1962, Gimson described the vowel of SQUARE as [ɛə]. The contemporary SQUARE vowel isn't lower than this, but has monophthongized to [ɛː]; see Chap. 13. However, publications on RP have generally used the symbol /eə/, suggesting a higher quality. To make it clear that SQUARE now has the [ɛ] quality and not [e], it has been included on the chart.

The diphthongs of FLEECE and FACE have widened, with lower starting qualities, nearer to [ɪ] and [ɛ]. Publications on RP have often ignored the diphthongal nature of FLEECE, routinely describing it as a monophthong, /iː/ (see Chap. 5). In rapid speech, of course, both FLEECE and FACE may indeed be monophthongized to qualities more like [i] and [e].

Backed Vowels

The diphthong of PRICE now begins with a backer quality than in RP (see Chap. 12). This quality could be transcribed as [ɑ] or [ʌ]; the latter is used in the *Routledge Dictionary of Pronunciation for Current English*, e.g. *price* /prʌɪs/, though this is potentially confusing, as the STRUT vowel is itself variable and not a clear reference point.

The vowel of STRUT has long been pronounced in a variety of ways. In earlier RP, it was quite central: the nineteenth century phonetician Henry Sweet used the symbol **a** for it. Generally speaking, a more back quality is now more common. In other words, the symbol /ʌ/ which Gimson chose is, if anything, now more accurate than it was.

Raised Vowels

The opener back vowels are higher in the vowel space than they were in RP. The long vowel of THOUGHT is nearer [o] than [ɔ], and the short vowel of LOT is nearer [ɔ] than [ɒ]. Daniel Jones used ɔ as the phoneme symbol for LOT, and this is phonetically appropriate today. For learners, it's worth noting that contemporary SSB THOUGHT is very like the 'o' of many languages, including Spanish and Japanese, but of course long. The LOT vowel, on the other hand, is still a good deal more open than international 'o'.

In Southern Britain the THOUGHT vowel is also the vowel of NORTH and FORCE. This makes *saw* and *sore* phonetically identical, **soː**, likewise *caught* and *court*, **koːt**. These words pairs are quite distinct in General American accents, where *saw*, *gnaw* and *caught* have more open pronunciations, and the *r* of *sore*, *nor* and *court* is pronounced (see Chap. 25).

The vowel of PALM and START is pronounced by many today with a higher tongue position than it was in RP. For such speakers it would be phonetically reasonable to use the symbol [ʌː]. However this book retains [ɑː] for this vowel because, as pointed out above, the STRUT vowel is variable and not a clear reference point. Although this suggests no change since RP, overall the articulation is less open than it was.

Centralized Vowels

The vowels of FOOT and CURE are now central, and the diphthongs of GOAT and GOOSE have central starting qualities. (For discussion of GOOSE's diphthongal nature, see Chap. 5.) All of these vowels previously had back articulations; the centralization of GOAT established itself early enough to be incorporated into Gimson's 1962 system, as /əʊ/. However, when dark /l/ follows, FOOT, GOAT and GOOSE all have more back articulations (CURE is never followed by dark /l/); see Chap. 6. Note that the CURE vowel is obsolescent; see Chap. 13.

Other Vowels

Located in the eye of the anti-clockwise storm, the mid-central vowels schwa and NURSE exhibit little change. Daniel Jones used the symbol ə: for NURSE, and Gimson's replacement of it with /ɜ:/ was phonetically unjustified. In fact, the symbol [ɜ] violated a guiding principle of phonetic transcription, 'one symbol, one sound', since it seems not to have been intended to indicate any significant difference in quality compared with schwa.

The vowel of KIT is only a little more open than it was, so the RP symbol /ɪ/ is still appropriate. However, the distribution of KIT has very much changed; see Chaps. 8 and 10. The quality /ɪ/ also survives in NEAR words, though the pronunciation of these words has altered in other ways; see Chap. 13.

MOUTH is the only vowel that has swum against the anti-clockwise current. Its typical starting quality was quite back in RP. Gimson chose the symbol /aʊ/ for it in 1962, though subsequent publications switched to /aʊ/. The starting point today is decidedly front, [a]; see Chap. 12.

A chart systematically comparing RP and modern values for the whole vowel system can be found on page 146.

Chapter 5

FLEECE, GOOSE and Other Diphthongs

In Brief Despite the familiar RP symbols /iː/ and /uː/, it's long been known that these two vowels are diphthongs, behaving like the other closing diphthongs of English. Their diphthongal character is now rather more pronounced than it was in RP. More accurate symbols are [ɪj] and [ʉw].

The FLEECE and GOOSE vowels, widely known as 'long i' and 'long u', occur in such common words as

- *east, green, even, people, previous, reader, recent, see, team, these, three, TV, week*
- *blue, Google, include, move, music, news, school, through, too/two, use, view, who*

As long ago as the nineteenth century, the phonetician Henry Sweet used the symbols **ij** and **uw** for these two vowels, which he termed 'semi-diphthongs'. His symbols reveal the 'falling' nature of the vowels, which begin strongly but end in a less sonorous glide.

There was a fashion among many speakers of RP for pronouncing FLEECE and GOOSE as long monophthongs, [iː] and [uː], but this now

© The Author(s) 2019
G. Lindsey, *English After RP*, https://doi.org/10.1007/978-3-030-04357-5_6

sounds old-fashioned, extremely so in the case of [uː]. Today, FLEECE and GOOSE are rather wider diphthongs than in Sweet's time. FLEECE tends to begin with a slightly more open quality, [ɪj], and GOOSE begins with a decidedly more front quality, [ʉw]; the final glide of the GOOSE diphthong may also be more front than true [w] for many speakers. These vowels are most diphthongal when they occur stressed at the end of a phrase, e.g. *Where can they be?* Or *I don't know what to do.*

Many non-natives can hear quite clearly that the modern GOOSE vowel sounds nothing like [uː] in native speech. I often hear non-natives trying to copy the modern GOOSE vowel by using something like the 'u' of French *rue* or the 'ü' of German *über*, which is a fairly reasonable attempt at [ʉw].

Another fashion among many RP speakers was to pronounce the end point of the FACE, PRICE and CHOICE diphthongs with a decidedly lax [ɪ], and the end point of MOUTH and GOAT with a lax [ʊ]. But in modern SSB we can hear, especially pre-pausally, that the end points of the glides are tenser. They can be transcribed as non-syllabic [i̯] and [u̯], or more simply as [j] and [w]: FACE as [ɛi̯] or [ɛj], PRICE as [ɑi̯] or [ɑj], MOUTH as [au̯] or [aw], etc.

Over the years numerous scholars have chosen to represent the end glides of diphthongs, naturally enough, with glide symbols. Such scholars typically include the FLEECE and GOOSE vowels among the diphthongs. For example:

FLEECE	ɪj	GOOSE	ʉw
FACE	ɛj	GOAT	əw
PRICE	ɑj	MOUTH	aw
CHOICE	oj		

There's no doubt that these seven vowels belong together, forming what phonologists call a 'natural class': they share properties which all other vowels lack. They're the vowels which may undergo a process known as smoothing (see Chap. 12). They're particularly subject to the effects of 'pre-fortis clipping' (shortening before voiceless consonants). They cannot be followed by linking /r/ (see Chap. 25). And they're the only vowels which **can** be immediately followed by another vowel:

neon	**nɪjɔn**	*ruin*	**rʉwɪn**
chaos	**kɛjɔs**	*poem*	**pəwɪm**
lion	**lɑjən**	*flower*	**flawə**
voyage	**vojɪdʒ**		

The fact that they inhibit a following linking consonant, but tolerate the presence of a following vowel, suggests that they end rather more like consonants than vowels; in other words, with glides. These glides act as separators, keeping the two syllables distinct in words like *chaos* and *voyage*.

Acknowledging that these vowels end in glides has practical benefits for the learner. For example, some of the words which are most commonly mispronounced by non-natives are ones in which weak FLEECE and GOOSE are followed by a vowel, such as *asso̲ciation* and *situ̲ation* (see Chaps. 8 and 9). In such words, non-natives very often fail to separate the two syllables in 'ua' and in 'ia'. But if the learner correctly pronounces the glides in these vowels, a more native-like pronunciation can be achieved: *si*[tʃʉw]*ation, asso*[sɪj]*ation*. The glides perform the same function when a vowel follows in the next word, e.g. *thr*[ɪj]*o'clock, val*[jʉw]*added*.

The RP symbols /eɪ/, /aɪ/, /ɔɪ/, /aʊ/, /əʊ/ are still used very widely. But they misrepresent modern SSB, in three ways. Firstly, they suggest that these vowels should be pronounced with lax end points, which is now old-fashioned. Secondly, they suggest that [ɪ] and [ʊ] are allowed word-finally and before vowels, which is no longer true; see Chaps. 8 and 9. Thirdly, they suggest that these five vowels are of a different type from FLEECE and GOOSE, whereas the seven vowels pattern together, constituting the set of closing diphthongs. If one insists on representing the end points of closing diphthongs with [ɪ] and [ʊ], it is in fact impossible to show transcriptionally that FLEECE and GOOSE belong to this set. For further discussion of vowel categories, see Chap. 13.

An objection is sometimes raised against the use of [j] and [w] rather than [ɪ] and [ʊ] to transcribe diphthongal glides, namely that we should not equate these glides with the initial glides of words like *yet* and *wet*. But the same objection applies at least as strongly to [ɪ] and [ʊ], since diphthongal glides should certainly not be equated with the vowels of

KIT and FOOT. A related objection is that diphthongal glides are not as forcefully articulated as the initial glides of *yet*, *wet*, etc. But greater force of articulation is exactly what we should expect of sounds in syllable onsets: compare the two plosives in *tent*. (Some scholars, in fact, argue that diphthongal glides can indeed be equated phonemically with the initial glides of *yet* and *wet*; but such arguments are beyond the scope of this book.)

Chapter 6

GOAT, GOOSE and FOOT Backing

In Brief In RP, the GOAT, GOOSE and FOOT vowels were essentially unaffected by a following dark /l/. In modern SSB, a following dark /l/ causes these three central vowels to be backed.

'GOOSE fronting' is often mentioned as a feature of contemporary English. This term is potentially misleading, in three ways. Firstly, the phenomenon is historic, not contemporary: GOOSE ceased to be a back vowel some time ago. Secondly, it wasn't a phenomenon specific to the GOOSE vowel: it applied to all four of the non-low back rounded vowels, GOAT, GOOSE, FOOT and CURE. Thirdly, it created not front vowels but central vowels.

The centralization of the RP GOAT vowel from [oʊ] to [əʊ] was established by the mid twentieth century. The centralization of GOOSE from [uː] or [ʊw] to [ʉw] began later, and the centralization of FOOT and CURE from [ʊ] and [ʊə] to [ɵ] and [ɵː] respectively seems somewhat more recent.

Contemporary GOOSE was described in Chap. 5. The FOOT vowel now sounds very like the vowel of French *je, le, que,* etc.; an appropriate IPA symbol for it is the 'barred o', [ɵ] (not to be confused with the symbols for schwa [ə] or the voiceless dental fricative [θ]).

© The Author(s) 2019
G. Lindsey, *English After RP*, https://doi.org/10.1007/978-3-030-04357-5_7

Historic centralization:

	Newer		Older
GOAT	ə	←	o
GOOSE	ʉ	←	u
FOOT, CURE	ɵ	←	ʊ

However, GOAT, GOOSE and FOOT are not always produced centrally. Before a dark /l/ [ɫ], their articulation is pulled back. (CURE never occurs before dark /l/.)

Contemporary backing:

	Basic		Before dark /l/
GOAT	ə	→	ɒ, ɔ
GOOSE	ʉ	→	u, o
FOOT	ɵ	→	ʊ, o

GOAT backing in words like *old, whole, told* and *goal* makes this vowel become more like the short LOT vowel; this is sometimes referred to as 'GOAT allophony'. Many speakers may fully replace the GOAT vowel with the LOT vowel in such words (see Chap. 7).

GOOSE and FOOT backing generally makes these vowels more like their old RP pronunciation, e.g. *pool* [puːɫ] or [pʊwɫ], *pull* [pʊɫ].

For many younger speakers, the backing of GOOSE merges it with the THOUGHT vowel, so that they use a quality in the region of [oː] and [uː] for both *pool* and *Paul*, *cool* and *call*, and *fool* and *fall*. (The singer-songwriter Ed Sheeran seems to be one of these speakers. In the song 'Thinking Out Loud', when he sings 'people fall in love', it sounds like 'people fool in love'.)

FOOT backing may also merge this vowel with THOUGHT, so there are speakers who pronounce *pool*, *Paul* and *pull* alike. While some of these speakers retain a following dark /l/, others exhibit /l/-vocalization (see Chap. 20).

Chapter 7

A LOT More Common

In Brief The vowel of LOT is now less open than in RP, [ɒ] > [ɔ]. It has widely replaced the THOUGHT vowel in words like *false* and *salt,* and for many speakers is replacing the GOAT vowel in words like *old* and *whole.*

The vowel of LOT (and *clock, got, not, Potter, quality, what,* etc.) is short, back and rounded. It's a distinctively Southern British vowel which General American lacks.

In RP, LOT was a very open vowel, produced with the tongue body low and back in the mouth. For this sound the IPA symbol [ɒ] was appropriate. Openness was a more important feature of this RP vowel than lip rounding, so that many RP speakers pronounced it as a short, unrounded [ɑ].

Over recent decades, the LOT vowel has risen in the vowel space, to become more like the typical open-mid vowel found in many languages, e.g. German *kommen*, Italian *posso*, Scottish English *Loch Ness,* Canadian English *Toronto.* The IPA symbol for this kind of vowel is [ɔ].

The cstablished RP symbols cause a good deal of confusion: the /ɔ:/ seen in British transcriptions misleads many people into thinking that

© The Author(s) 2019
G. Lindsey, *English After RP*, https://doi.org/10.1007/978-3-030-04357-5_8

the IPA symbol [ɔ] represents a sound like the SSB THOUGHT vowel, but that is now closer to [oː] (see Chap. 4).

Although LOT has raised, it has **not** become the mid 'o' vowel of very many languages, such as Spanish and Japanese. Speakers of these languages still need to make LOT more open than their 'o'.

The LOT vowel has not only changed in quality. Its distribution has also changed, so that it's heard increasingly in words where RP had the THOUGHT or GOAT vowels.

THOUGHT > LOT words

These words have /l/ followed by a consonant: mainly /t/, sometimes /s/ or /d/. The change is more established in frequently used words, e.g. *halt* and *salt,* and less common in rarer words, like *cauldron.*

Examples:
alter, alteration, alternative, assault, Baltic, cauldron, false, falsify, fault, faulty, Gibraltar, halt, malt, Malden, Maldives, Malta, salt, vault, Walter

GOAT > LOT words

These words, with a syllable-final dark /l/, had the GOAT diphthong /əʊ/ in RP. Today, SSB speakers usually have GOAT backing in this context. This means that they shift the first part of the diphthong from schwa [ə] to the quality of the LOT vowel, creating [ɔʊ] or [ɔw]; some transcribe this as [ɒʊ], referring to the shift as 'GOAT allophony'. See Chap. 6.

Increasingly, younger speakers simply use the short LOT vowel [ɔ] in these words.

Examples:
bold, bolt, bowl, coal, cold, control, fold, goal, gold, hold, hole, holster, mould, old, patrol, poll, poultry, role/roll, shoulder, soldier, sole/soul, stroll, told, troll, volt, whole

Chapter 8

KIT: Still Going Strong (but happY Never Existed)

In Brief RP used short-lax [ɪ] in many contexts. Today it occurs only before consonants. Elsewhere it's been replaced with the long-tense FLEECE vowel or, in closing diphthongs, with a glide, [i̯] or [j].

In RP, short-lax [ɪ] was used in a wide range of contexts. As an independent strong vowel, it occurred in thousands of words where it remains essentially unchanged today. A handful of the most common are *big, Britain, click, England, film, image, link, little, picture, system, thing, Twitter, video, women*. Note that it's always followed by a consonant in such words.

RP also used [ɪ] in thousands of words where it's now old-fashioned. There are three relevant contexts:

1. Immediately before a vowel, e.g. *associate, oriental, polyester, previous, reality, Romeo, studying, various*
2. Word-finally, e.g. *city, coffee, happy, money, movie, only, recipe, taxi, very*
3. As the end point of the diphthongs FACE /eɪ/, PRICE /aɪ/ and CHOICE /ɔɪ/, e.g. *day, face, they; high, price, try; boy, choice, employ*

© The Author(s) 2019
G. Lindsey, *English After RP*, https://doi.org/10.1007/978-3-030-04357-5_9

All three of these contexts, and not just the first, resulted in the placing of [ɪ] immediately before another vowel. For example:

studying	/ˈstʌdɪɪŋ/
happy enough	/ˈhæpɪˈnʌf/
my experience	/ˈmaɪɪkˈspɪərɪəns/

(Note that the RP transcription /ɪə/ was ambiguous, as it could stand for either a centring diphthong or a two-syllable sequence of /ɪ/ plus schwa.)

Modern SSB does not use [ɪ] in these contexts. So we can say that modern speech prohibits [ɪ] in any context that would allow a vowel to follow directly.

Generally, English does not allow lax vowels to occur before other vowels. There are no words of English in which /ʌ/, for example, occurs before another vowel. It was a peculiarity of RP to allow lax [ɪ] (and also [ʊ]) to do so, a peculiarity that has now been eliminated. The use of /ɪ/ in phrase-final position, in words like *coffee, happy* and *movie,* is now perceived as distinctly old-fashioned, or a regionalism.

In contexts 1. and 2., SSB speakers today use the FLEECE vowel, e.g. /ˈhæpiː/ **ˈhapɪj**. The process by which FLEECE replaced KIT in these contexts is widely referred to as 'happY tensing'. However, very few publications show the change to FLEECE as such. Several decades ago, during the period when KIT was being replaced by FLEECE, a fashion arose for using a non-phonemic symbol /i/ to indicate the transitional variability, older speakers using /ɪ/ and younger speakers using /iː/. The presence in many resources of an extra symbol /i/ has led to widespread belief in a specific 'happY vowel', but such a vowel never existed. And now that /ɪ/ is no longer recommendable in these contexts, the symbol /i/ has rather lost its point and tends merely to cause confusion.

In context 2., some speakers use /ɪ/ when a suffix consonant is added. Such speakers have *movie* **ˈmʉwvɪj**, but *movies* **ˈmʉwvɪz**.

In closing diphthongs (context 3.), modern speech uses a glide to a tenser end point, which can be transcribed as non-syllabic [i̯] or more simply as [j]; see Chap. 5. There's a practical advantage in pronunciation teaching if diphthongal glides are shown as such before a vowel, as this encourages good separation of syllables:

studying	ˈstʌdɪjɪŋ
happy enough	ˈhapɪjɪˈnʌf
my experience	mɑjɪkˈspɪːrɪjən(t)s

In weak syllables, the KIT vowel survives today only when a consonant follows, e.g. *important, office, pages, public, Spanish, united*. But there's a gradual tendency, in an increasing number of words, for weak KIT to be interchangeable with, or replaced by, schwa /ə/. This is known as weak vowel merger; see Chap. 10.

Chapter 9

FOOT: Even Rarer, but Still Common

In Brief The FOOT vowel /ʊ/ was very widespread in RP, as it occurred in many weak syllables. It's now rarer in weak syllables, but the small number of words with strong FOOT are very frequently used. Its modern pronunciation is central, [ɵ].

Over time, the occurrence of the FOOT vowel /ʊ/ has become ever more restricted. In Shakespeare's time (Early Modern English), /ʊ/ occurred as a strong vowel in many words including *cup, cut, dust, hundred, jump, mud, number, run, rush, summer, stuck*. The first great restriction on the occurrence of /ʊ/ was the FOOT-STRUT split, which changed /ʊ/ to /ʌ/ in hundreds of such words.

The older pronunciations are retained by speakers in the north of England, who still say /kʊt/, /kʊp/, /dʊst/, /ˈhʊndrəd/ etc. In the South, the strong vowel /ʊ/ was kept in only a relatively small number of words, e.g. *bush, full, put*, where it survives today; see below for a more complete list.

© The Author(s) 2019
G. Lindsey, *English After RP*, https://doi.org/10.1007/978-3-030-04357-5_10

RP also used [ʊ] in many other words where it's now old-fashioned. There are three relevant contexts:

1. Immediately before a vowel, e.g. *gen<u>u</u>ine, grad<u>u</u>ate, infl<u>u</u>ence, sit<u>u</u>ation, stat<u>u</u>esque*
2. Word-finally in a few words, e.g. *contin<u>ue</u>, int<u>o</u>, thank y<u>ou</u>*
3. As the end point of the diphthongs GOAT /əʊ/ and MOUTH /aʊ/, e.g. *bel<u>ow</u>, g<u>oa</u>t, n<u>o</u>; h<u>ow</u>, m<u>ou</u>th, pl<u>ough</u>*

All three of these contexts, and not just the first, resulted in the placing of [ʊ] immediately before a vowel. For example:

influence	/ˈɪnflʊəns/
go ahead	/ˈgəʊəˈhed/
how unusual	/ˈhaʊʌnˈjuːʒʊəl/

(Note that the RP transcription /ʊə/ was ambiguous, as it could stand for either a centring diphthong or a two-syllable sequence of /ʊ/ plus schwa.)

Modern standard speech does not use [ʊ] in these contexts. Generally, English does not allow lax vowels like /ʌ/ to occur before another vowel. It was a peculiarity of RP to allow the lax vowels [ɪ] and [ʊ] to do so, a peculiarity that has now been eliminated. The use of /ʊ/ phrase-finally in words like *continue* and *thank you* is now perceived as old-fashioned.

In contexts 1. and 2., SSB speakers today use the GOOSE vowel, e.g. /ˈθæŋkjuː/ ˈθaŋkjʉw. However, very few publications show the GOOSE vowel in context 1. Several decades ago, during the period when FOOT was being replaced by GOOSE in such words, a fashion arose for using a non-phoneme symbol /u/ to indicate the transitional variability, older speakers using /ʊ/ and younger speakers using /uː/. But now that /ʊ/ is no longer recommendable in these contexts, the symbol /u/ has rather lost its point.

In closing diphthongs (context 3.), modern speech uses a glide to a tenser quality, which can be transcribed as non-syllabic [u̯] or more simply as [w]; see Chap. 5. There's a practical advantage in pronunciation teaching if diphthongal glides are shown as such before a vowel, as it encourages good separation of syllables:

influence	ˈɪnflʉwən(t)s
go ahead	ˈgəwəˈhɛd
how unusual	ˈhawʌnˈjʉʒʉwəl

In weak syllables, the FOOT vowel survives today only when a consonant follows, e.g. *ed<u>u</u>cation, partic<u>u</u>lar, pop<u>u</u>lar*. But there's a tendency to replace weak /ʊ/ with schwa /ə/ (see Chap. 10). This means that for some speakers, the FOOT vowel is exclusively a strong vowel.

As described in Chap. 6, the contemporary FOOT vowel is central; an appropriate IPA symbol for it is the 'barred o', [ɵ]. Although the number of English words containing the FOOT vowel has shrunk drastically, most of the words in which it robustly survives are very frequently used. Learners of English will benefit from memorizing them:

- *bull, bullet, bulletin, bully, bush, butcher, full, fulfil, pudding, pull, pulley, pulpit, push, pussy, put, cushion, sugar*
- *book, brook, cook, crook, hook, look, nook, rook, shook, took*
- *good, hood, stood, wood*
- *foot, soot, Tootsie*
- *wolf, woman, woof, wool, Worcester* /ˈwʊstə/ **ˈwɵstə**
- *couldn't, wouldn't, shouldn't* (the positive forms *could, would, should* are usually weak: /kəd/, /wəd/, /ʃəd/)

FOOT also occurs in words containing those listed above, such as *Brooklyn, childhood, football, overlook, pullover, understood, Worcestershire*, and in some words of foreign origin like *B<u>u</u>ddhist, co<u>u</u>rier, Istanb<u>u</u>l, K<u>u</u>shner, L<u>u</u>dwig, M<u>o</u>slem*.

Chapter 10

Weak Vowel Merger

In Brief RP used the KIT and FOOT vowels very widely in weak syllables. Before consonants, they're increasingly interchangeable with, or replaced by, schwa /ə/. This is further advanced with FOOT than with KIT.

RP made extensive use of the KIT vowel /ɪ/ and the FOOT vowel /ʊ/ in weak syllables before consonants. There's an increasing tendency to replace these with schwa. This is known as weak vowel merger, and is well established in American English.

In SSB, weak vowel merger is more advanced with words which had weak /ʊ/ in RP, often preceded by /j/. Examples include *amb<u>u</u>lance*, *artic<u>u</u>late*, *ed<u>u</u>cation*, *partic<u>u</u>lar*, *pop<u>u</u>lation*, *stim<u>u</u>late*. In all such words, schwa is now common and recommendable to the learner, e.g. *particular* **pə'tɪkjələ**.

In the case of RP's weak /ɪ/, many words are now widely heard with /ə/ instead, e.g. the second vowels of *for<u>ei</u>gn* and *arb<u>i</u>trary*. But there are many words which firmly retain /ɪ/ for most SSB speakers. A well-known word pair is *Lenin* and *Lennon*, which are typically merged in America but still distinct in SSB: *Lenin* has /ɪ/ and *Lennon* has /ə/. Affixes written

© The Author(s) 2019
G. Lindsey, *English After RP*, https://doi.org/10.1007/978-3-030-04357-5_11

with 'i' are typically pronounced with /ɪ/, e.g. the prefixes *dis-, in-, im-, mis-* and the endings *-ic, -id, -ing, -ish*.

There are many other pairs of words which are distinguished in pronunciation by the contrast between /ɪ/ and /ə/. For most SSB speakers, the endings *-es* and *-ers* are /ɪz/ and /əz/ respectively. So we have /ɪz/ in words such as *teaches* and *manages,* but /əz/ in *teachers* and *managers.* The same applies to words ending *-ed* and *-ered*, so we have /ɪd/ in words such as *counted* and *tended*, but /əd/ in words such as *countered* and *tendered*.

In some words, /ɪ/ and /ə/ have long been interchangeable. These include the weak prefixes *be-, de-, pre-* and *re-*. Note that there are some speakers who now use the FLEECE vowel in these prefixes, the same change that has occurred in the pre-vocalic and potentially pre-vocalic contexts described in Chap. 8 (known widely as 'happY tensing').

In a range of endings written with 'e', RP had /ɪ/, while contemporary speakers increasingly use /ə/:

-et, e.g. *interpret, magnet, Margaret, tablet, secret*
-est, e.g. *latest, biggest*
-less, e.g. *regardless, wireless*
-ness, e.g. *business, fitness, illness, witness*
-red, e.g. *Alfred, hatred, sacred*
-ress, e.g. *actress, mattress, waitress*

The noun/adjective ending *-ate* was /ɪt/ in RP, but this has now mostly been replaced with /ət/. Common examples are *appropriate, candidate, chocolate, corporate, delicate, desperate, graduate, immediate, intimate, passionate, separate, ultimate.* However, in two-syllable words like *climate, private, senate,* /ɪ/ may still be heard. (In verbs, the ending *-ate* has the strong FACE vowel, e.g. *to appropriate, to separate,* but learners should avoid putting the main stress on it, as they often do.)

Chapter 11

Two Kinds of BATH

In Brief A number of words have the PALM vowel in the south of England, but the TRAP vowel in the north of England and in North America. The TRAP pronunciations were not acceptable as RP, but today they're a standard variant.

The contrast between the TRAP vowel and the PALM vowel is made in Southern British, North American and many other varieties of English. Learners should make sure that they differentiate the vowels in *gather* and *father*, *gamma* and *Obama*; these pairs contain the TRAP and PALM vowels respectively.

However, there are many words like *bath, after, ask, answer*, which are variable. These words have TRAP in some varieties of English, and PALM in others. North Americans generally use the TRAP vowel, /æsk/, /bæθ/, while RP was strict in using the PALM vowel in such words, e.g. /ɑːsk/, /bɑːθ/.

The RP pronunciations arose in the south of England in the eighteenth century. Everyday words like *bath, ask* and *answer* underwent a process

© The Author(s) 2019
G. Lindsey, *English After RP*, https://doi.org/10.1007/978-3-030-04357-5_12

widely known as 'BATH-broadening'. This 'broadened' the short TRAP vowel into the long PALM vowel:

- before the voiceless fricatives /θ/, /f/, /s/, e.g. *bath, after, ask*
- before a nasal and a following consonant, e.g. *answer, demand*

BATH-broadening did not apply to more technical words like *maths, graph* and *mass,* which retained the TRAP vowel. But in many cases it's hard to say why some words broadened, like *chant* and *sample*, while others didn't, like *pant* and *trample.*

So the pronunciation with the TRAP vowel dates back further. The British settlement of America began well before BATH-broadening happened, so General American speakers lack it, as do millions of speakers in the north of England.

These differences still exist, but **social** changes have taken place in Britain. Throughout most of the twentieth century, RP occupied such a special position of privilege and prestige that deviations from it were looked down on in many walks of life. Official BBC announcers and newsreaders, for example, were expected to be strict RP speakers, with BATH-broadening.

Today greater diversity is allowed, even among BBC newsreaders, documentary narrators, etc. It's now common for such speakers to have un-broadened TRAP in *bath, after, ask, answer, demand, chant, sample,* etc. We might say that SSB now includes un-broadened BATH words as an option.

This is convenient for learners aiming at a British accent, as BATH-broadening can be tricky to learn. Not only is it hard to explain why words did or did not broaden; there are also words which have broadened more recently, such as *graph*. It's no longer a high priority for learners to use the broadened forms.

For those who do wish to use broadened forms in the right words, lists of common examples follow:

Words with the PALM vowel in the south of England:
advance, after, Alexander, answer, ask, basket, casket, cast, chance, chant, class, demand, example, fast, Flanders, flask, glass, grant, graph, laugh, last, master, pass, past, path, plant, sample, Sanders, Sandra, slander, slant, staff, task

Words with the TRAP vowel in the south of England:

Alaska, Amanda, Anderson, ample, asthma, Basque, cancel, cancer, classic, decaf, elastic, fancy, gas, gander, gasket, grand, graphic, land, manned, mass, maths, Miranda, panda, pander, pant, pants, pasta, plastic, rant, sand, trample, transfer, transit

Chapter 12

PRICE and MOUTH

In Brief In RP, the first part of the PRICE diphthong was rather front, while many speakers gave the first part of the MOUTH diphthong a back quality. Today, PRICE begins further back and MOUTH further forward.

In Chap. 4, we saw that the large number of vowel changes in Southern Britain since RP together make up a grand 'anti-clockwise' shift in the vowel space. One of these changes was the backing of the PRICE diphthong from RP's [aɪ] to the contemporary pronunciations [ɑj] or [ʌj].

One vowel change has been in the opposite direction. This is the fronting of the MOUTH diphthong. In RP this was for many speakers [ɑʊ] (the symbol chosen for the phoneme by Gimson in 1962), whereas the contemporary pronunciation is [aw], beginning with a front quality. We can say that the starting qualities of PRICE and MOUTH have switched since RP.

This switch has brought today's SSB closer to the traditional majority pronunciation of the London area: London's working class Cockneys had a front quality in MOUTH and a back quality in PRICE. (On the other hand, a more front pronunciation of PRICE can be heard today from

© The Author(s) 2019
G. Lindsey, *English After RP*, https://doi.org/10.1007/978-3-030-04357-5_13

younger people who speak 'Multicultural London English'. MLE, said to be replacing Cockney in London, is beyond the scope of this book.)

Smoothing

The most established symbols for PRICE and MOUTH are /aɪ/ and /aʊ/, suggesting that these two diphthongs begin with the same quality. For many RP speakers this was the case.

When PRICE, MOUTH and the other closing diphthongs were followed by schwa /ə/, RP speakers could apply 'smoothing', which removed the second part of the diphthong. As a result, many RP speakers could pronounce *tire* /taɪə/ and *tower* /taʊə/ identically, as [taə].

Merging words like *tire* and *tower* in this way now sounds old-fashioned. Today PRICE and MOUTH have clearly different starting qualities, which they maintain even when affected by smoothing.

Smoothing of a diphthong + schwa is still a widespread process in contemporary speech, but it works in a somewhat different way from RP's smoothing. Today, smoothing simply creates a long monophthong out of the diphthong's first element. For example, *tire* [tɑjə] can become [tɑː], and *tower* [tawə] can become [taː]. Modern smoothing occurs most often before before dark /l/ and before linking /r/. For example:

child	[tʃɑjəɫd]	→	[tʃɑːɫd]
fire alarm	[fɑjə] + [əˈlɑːm]	→	[fɑːrəˈlɑːm]
an hour and a half	[awə] + [ən]	→	*an* [aːrən] *a half*

Contemporary smoothing creates monophthongs, whereas the old RP smoothing created centring diphthongs. As the next chapter explains, centring diphthongs are steadily being eliminated from contemporary speech.

Chapter 13

The Decline of the Centring Diphthongs

In Brief Although most dictionaries are full of the symbols /ɪə/, /eə/, /ʊə/, the centring diphthongs of RP are rarely heard today. These are increasingly replaced with long monophthongs, [ɪː], [ɛː], [əː], [oː].

Twentieth century RP featured four centring diphthongs, /ɪə/, /eə/, /ɔə/ and /ʊə/. These all involved a glide from the edge of the vowel space towards the centre. They arose due to the loss of a following /r/ in Southern Britain in the period just before RP arose, around the turn of the nineteenth century.

There's been a steady tendency for them to be lost. It is in fact possible to describe today's SSB entirely without centring diphthongs.

FORCE /ɔə/ and CURE /ʊə/

These two centring diphthongs were increasingly replaced by the THOUGHT-NORTH monophthong during the twentieth century, /ɔə/ declining more rapidly than /ʊə/. Transcriptions with /ɔə/ were included in the *English Pronouncing Dictionary* as recently as

© The Author(s) 2019
G. Lindsey, *English After RP*, https://doi.org/10.1007/978-3-030-04357-5_14

1977, but today's dictionaries have dropped /ɔə/, and the switch to THOUGHT-NORTH can be considered complete. This means that all words which once had /ɔə/, like *board*, *force*, *more*, now have the THOUGHT-NORTH vowel /ɔː/, in contemporary pronunciation [oː]. So *hoarse*, once /hɔəs/, is now pronounced the same as *horse*, /hɔːs/ **hoːs**.

The CURE diphthong /ʊə/ is following the same path. For a long time, words have been switching their preferred pronunciation from /ʊə/ to the THOUGHT-NORTH vowel. Some of the earlier words to change were *poor*, *sure*, *your*. More recent examples of words pronounced widely or mainly with THOUGHT-NORTH include *mourn*, *tourist*, and the word *cure* itself.

Today's learners may safely use THOUGHT-NORTH in any word which they see transcribed with /ʊə/. However, not all speakers have made the switch in all words. In words where the sound /r/ follows, e.g. *during*, *Europe*, *security*, many speakers use central monophthongs, [əː] or [ʉː]. Phonemically, these might be analysed as forms of the GOOSE vowel, or else as a modern, monophthongized CURE vowel. But the sound [ʊə] is heard rarely today.

Some speakers can give CURE words a two-syllable pronunciation, with GOOSE plus schwa; these speakers may also smooth this into [ʉː] or [əː], by the smoothing process described in the previous chapter. For example, we might hear from the same speaker *secure* **sɪˈkjʉwə** and *security* **sɪˈkjəːrɪtɪj**.

SQUARE /eə/

This centring diphthong has undergone a process of monophthongization since RP, so that it's now very widely produced as a long [ɛː], e.g. *square* **skwɛː**, *there* **ðɛː**, *where* and *wear* **wɛː**. A few publications have adopted the symbol /ɛː/ in place of the old /eə/, including the *Routledge Dictionary of Pronunciation for Current English*.

This is the same quality as the short DRESS vowel /e/, which is now [ɛ]. So it's important for learners aiming at an SSB accent to master the length difference between e.g. *shed* ʃɛd and *shared* ʃɛːd. (Many will find it easier to pronounce the *r* in SQUARE words, as American, Scottish and Irish speakers do.)

Retaining a centring diphthong [eə] or [ɛə] is characteristic of a broad London area accent.

NEAR /ɪə/

This centring diphthong has changed in two ways. One change, which began decades ago, was the tensing of the first part. This became more like the FLEECE vowel, resulting in [iːə] or [ɪjə], potentially two syllables. As a result *career,* traditionally /kəˈrɪə/ in RP, became like *Korea,* /kəˈriːə/ **kəˈrɪjə**.

The other change is a smoothing process, which results in a long monophthong [ɪː]. (This can be seen as an example of the same modern smoothing process discussed in the previous chapter.) The monophthong [ɪː] is today the usual pronunciation when /r/ follows, as it often does, e.g. *appearance*, RP /əˈpɪərəns/, contemporary **əˈpɪːrən(t)s**. Other words with [ɪː] before /r/ include *experience, interior, material, period, serious, series.* (Alternatively, some speakers switch to the FLEECE vowel in such words.)

For many speakers, [ɪː] is established in the basic pronunciation of *here* and *year,* the two most commonly used NEAR words, **hɪː, jɪː.** Younger speakers increasingly use [ɪː] in other NEAR words too: *clear, appear, idea,* etc.

Although most publications retain the RP symbol /ɪə/, this does not phonetically represent contemporary speech. A true diphthong gliding from [ɪ] to [ə] is relatively rare.

Vowel Categories

The vowels of English are clearly grouped into several categories. The vowels in each category share phonetic and phonological characteristics which those in the other categories lack. Comparing RP with contemporary standard speech, we see that the categories are essentially unchanged; but changes in pronunciation over recent decades have served to reinforce the categories, making the vowels within them even more alike.

However, the vowel symbols proposed for RP by Gimson in 1962, which have been become so established in books and in people's minds, actually obscure the real categories. They suggest the division of the long vowels into these two categories:

* iː ɑː ɜː ɔː uː
* eɪ aɪ ɔɪ aʊ əʊ ɪə eə ʊə

But this was not even appropriate for RP. The real categorization of the long RP vowels was as follows:

* iː eɪ aɪ ɔɪ aʊ əʊ uː
* ɪə eə ɑː ɜː ɔː ʊə

The first group, as we saw in Chap. 5, constitute the closing diphthongs. Despite the symbols /iː/ and /uː/, the diphthongal nature of FLEECE and GOOSE was known at least as far back as the work of Henry Sweet. The seven vowels in this group are also the only ones which permit an immediately following vowel, and they're never followed by linking /r/. They're particularly subject to the effects of 'pre-fortis clipping' and they sometimes undergo 'pre-l breaking' before dark /l/. And they're the vowels which may undergo 'smoothing' when followed by schwa (see Chap. 12).

By contrast, the members of the second group are never followed by another vowel within a morpheme. If followed by a vowel at the start of the next word, they're typically separated from it by a linking /r/ or by a glottal stop. Therefore, they never undergo smoothing before schwa. And they're less susceptible than the members of the first group to pre-l breaking pre-fortis clipping.

Pronunciation changes since RP have served only to reinforce the true groupings. FLEECE and GOOSE have become somewhat more diphthongal than they were in RP, making those two vowels even more like the other members of their group. And, as we've just seen, the decline of the centring diphthongs means that the second group is fast becoming (for many speakers has already become) the set of long monophthongs.

We can make these facts explicit by transcribing the vowels with phonetically accurate and phonologically insightful symbols:

- ɪj ɛj ɑj oj aw əw ʉw
- ɪː ɛː ɑː əː oː ɵː

A full vowel chart with these symbols, and the traditional RP symbols for comparison, can be found on p. 146.

Part III

Consonants

Chapter 14

More Aspiration (and Affrication)

In Brief Aspiration of /p/, /t/ and /k/ was said to be restricted to stressed syllables in RP. It's now general, except after fricatives, especially /s/. In the case of /t/, the plosive is generally affricated, [tˢ].

The aspiration of English /p/, /t/ and /k/ refers to devoicing at the beginning of a following sound, typically creating an /h/-like whisper, e.g. *kiss* [kʰɪs]. It's important for speakers of languages without aspiration, like French and Spanish, to learn how to aspirate /p/, /t/ and /k/ in English.

RP had less aspiration than contemporary SSB. Many RP speakers had rather brief aspiration periods, i.e. a short 'voice onset time'. For some RP speakers this was true even in strongly stressed syllables. And unstressed syllables were not regarded as aspirated in RP.

For speakers today, short or weak aspiration is one of the features of old RP that makes it sound old-fashioned; comedians may use it to make fun of 'posh' speakers of the past. Additionally, /p/, /t/ and /k/ in unstressed syllables now clearly have longer voice onset times than the unaspirated plosives of languages like French and Spanish. In *carpet*, for example, neither the /k/ nor the /p/ has the very short voice onset time of Spanish *casa* or *padre*. Similarly, the /k/ in the noun *take-off* will typically have aspiration, so that the end may sound very like *cough*.

© The Author(s) 2019
G. Lindsey, *English After RP*, https://doi.org/10.1007/978-3-030-04357-5_15

Aspiration is typically longer in stressed syllables, but learners should make sure they can produce aspiration in /p/, /t/ and /k/, regardless of stress.

The alveolar plosive /t/ differs somewhat from /p/ and /k/, in that it's generally released into a period of /s/-like friction. This is called 'affrication', and can be transcribed as [tˢ]. Affrication is also common with /d/, producing [dᶻ]. Affrication was less noticeable in RP, but in contemporary speech it's common in both stressed and unstressed syllables; it can be heard both in words like *tea* and in words like *city*. This differentiates SSB pronunciation from American pronunciation, which has 'flapping' (or 'tapping') in words like *city*. Some SSB speakers have quite extreme affrication, so that *city* can sound very like *sissy*.

The only context in which /p/, /t/ and /k/ are never aspirated, or affricated, is when preceded by a fricative in the same basic word (morpheme). The clusters written 'sp', 'st' and 'sk' or 'sc' contain unaspirated plosives which sound like English /b/, /d/ and /g/. For example, the word *Spanish* sounds like *banish* preceded by /s/; *stay* sounds like *day* preceded by /s/; and *screen* sounds like *green* preceded by /s/. Many proficient non-native users of English make the mistake of aspirating /p/, /t/ and /k/ in such words.

Phonemically, we could analyse such words as containing /sb/, /sd/ and /sg/. If we did so, it would be possible make the simple claim that English /p/, /t/ and /k/ are **always** aspirated. However, the transcriptions /sb/, /sd/ and /sg/ would lead many learners to mispronounce them as [zb], [zd] and [zg], which is at least as incorrect as using aspirated [pʰ] in *Spanish*.

Aspiration is also disallowed after other fricatives within a morpheme, though there are fewer examples. So in *after*, *-ter* typically sounds like *-der* in *ladder*, not like *-ter* in *later*.

Ejectives

In word-final position, /p/, /t/ and /k/ are sometimes heard today in a strengthened form that wasn't characteristic of RP. This is the realization of these three plosives as **ejectives**, [p'], [t'] and [k'].

Ejectives involve making a glottal stop during the oral closure, and forcefully raising the larynx in the throat. This compresses the air in the mouth so that a very sharp sound is heard when the oral closure is released.

Ejective articulation is most common with /k/ at the end of a phrase, as in *next wee<u>k</u>, on Facebo<u>ok</u>, what would you li<u>ke</u>?*

Chapter 15

/tʃ/ and /dʒ/: A New *si-chew-ation*

In Brief RP's consonant clusters /tj/ and /dj/ are increasingly replaced by /tʃ/ and /dʒ/ in SSB. This is more common in weak syllables, e.g. e*du*cation, but is increasingly heard also in stressed syllables, e.g. *Tuesday*.

The consonant clusters /tj/ and /dj/ were very common in RP, occurring in words like *situation, perpetual, tune, Tuesday*, and *due, during, education, gradual*.

Over time, there's been a tendency for such two-consonant clusters to coalesce into the single affricate consonants /tʃ/ and /dʒ/. The process is widely known as 'palatalization' or 'yod coalescence', 'yod' being the name for the sound /j/.

Coalescence had already happened to some words by the time of RP, e.g. *culture, future, picture*, and *soldier*. In most other cases, RP insisted on /tj/ and /dj/, although other, less prestigious accents used yod coalescence more widely. Writing in the early 1980s, phonetician John Wells said of words like *situation* that 'in England the /tʃ/ pronunciation is felt to be rather vulgar' (*Accents of English*, p. 247).

Since then, yod coalescence has become widespread, and the negative attitude of some older speakers towards pronunciations like ˌsɪtʃʉwˈɛjʃən is no longer relevant for the learner.

© The Author(s) 2019
G. Lindsey, *English After RP*, https://doi.org/10.1007/978-3-030-04357-5_16

The clusters /tj/ and /dj/ have by no means disappeared, surviving more robustly in stressed syllables. But the /tʃ/ and /dʒ/ forms are well enough established for the *Cambridge English Pronouncing Dictionary* to list /tʃ/ and /dʒ/ as the first pronunciations for words including *Tuesday, tuna, tune, tuition, tutor, YouTube*, and *dual, due, duplicate, durable, during, duty*.

Suit, pursuit, Etc.

The other RP clusters involving alveolar consonants and yod, /sj/ and /zj/, behave rather differently in SSB. At the beginning of a word, /sj/ has been simplified to /s/ by most speakers, with /j/ lost altogether in words like *suit, suitable, super, supermarket, supervise*. Non-initially, some speakers have coalesced /sj/ and /zj/ into /ʃ/ and /ʒ/, but very many speakers retain /sj/ in words like *assume* and *pursue*, and /zj/ in words like *presume*.

Chapter 16

/tʃ/ and /dʒ/: A New *chrend*

In Brief RP allowed postalveolar /r/ to form clusters with the alveolar stops /t/ and /d/, but not with the postalveolar stops /tʃ/ and /dʒ/. Many speakers now use all-postalveolar clusters: /tʃr/, /dʒr/.

The English /r/, different from the /r/ of most languages, is a postalveolar approximant [ɹ]. This means it's articulated with the tongue just behind the alveolar ridge, a little further back than for alveolar sounds like /t/, /d/, /n/ and /s/.

This postalveolar /r/ forms clusters with the similarly postalveolar fricative /ʃ/, but not with the alveolar fricative /s/. So we have words like *shrink*, *shred* and *shrug*, but no words like *srink, *sred and *srug. This is why English speakers generally pronounce the name written *Sri Lanka* with /ʃ/, as if it were *Shri Lanka*. It's easier to produce an all-postalveolar cluster /ʃr/ than an alveolar-then-postalveolar cluster /sr/.

RP did have clusters of alveolar and postalveolar phonemes, namely /tr/ as in *trade, train, travel, trend, trip*, and /dr/ as in *drama, dream, dress, drink, drive*. Typically, the tip of the tongue was retracted for the /t/ or /d/ in anticipation of the postalveolar /r/, resulting in [tɹ] and [dɹ]. In addition, friction was often produced during the /r/, creating phonetic affricates. However, speakers still considered them to be sequences of /t/ and /d/ plus /r/.

© The Author(s) 2019
G. Lindsey, *English After RP*, https://doi.org/10.1007/978-3-030-04357-5_17

Such pronunciations are still common. But a new trend has developed in both Britain and America, eliminating alveolar-postalveolar clusters altogether. Speakers of this type avoid not only /sr/ but also /tr/ and /dr/, replacing /tr/ and /dr/ with the all-postalveolar clusters /tʃr/ and /dʒr/. These clusters are similar to [tɹ] and [dɹ], but whereas [tɹ] and [dɹ] typically have a more 'apical' articulation, with the tongue tip curled up, /tʃr/ and /dʒr/ typically have a more 'laminal' articulation, with a more convex tongue shape; users definitely feel them to be sequences of /tʃ/ and /dʒ/ plus /r/.

For such speakers, *trip* and *truck* are **tʃrɪp** and **tʃrʌk**, while *drip* and *drunk* are **dʒrɪp** and **dʒrʌŋk**.

When a written *s* precedes, it may also be given a postalveolar pronunciation, resulting in the all-postalveolar cluster **ʃtʃr**. This means that *strip* and *struck* may be heard as **ʃtʃrɪp** and **ʃtʃrʌk**.

Although these transcriptions look less like the written forms of these words, in terms of phonetics and phonology the change to all-postalveolar clusters is a simplification and regularization.

Chapter 17

Epen-t-thesis

In Brief RP generally made a distinction between words like *prince* and *prints, Thomson* and *Thompson.* Today many speakers pronounce such pairs the same, as a result of an 'epenthetic' plosive introduced into words like *prince* and *Thomson.*

Traditionally, many words of English contain a nasal consonant followed by a fricative. An example would be *prince*, /prɪns/. The /n/ is a stop sound, which means that the oral airflow of speech is stopped; the tongue blade is held against the alveolar ridge while breath is re-directed through the nose. As /n/ changes to /s/, airflow must be switched from nasal to oral, and at the same time the stoppage at the alveolar ridge must be released. If the second of these events happens a little late, there's a brief period in which both nasal and oral airflow are stopped. This is a brief oral stop or plosive at the same place of articulation as the nasal, creating in this case [prɪnts], which may be indistinguishable from *prints*.

The appearance of such extra sounds is called 'epenthesis'. The extra sounds themselves are called 'epenthetic' sounds.

Epenthesis of an oral stop between a nasal and a fricative is very natural. Many speakers do it on some occasions but not others; the epenthetic stop may be so brief as to be barely noticeable, or it may clearly be a

© The Author(s) 2019
G. Lindsey, *English After RP*, https://doi.org/10.1007/978-3-030-04357-5_18

fully-fledged plosive consonant. Epenthesis is more likely if the fricative after the nasal is voiceless, when the articulatory system has an additional voicing change to handle. It's less likely if the fricative is at the beginning of a stressed syllable, e.g. *in'sane.*

Epenthetic stops are most commonly alveolar, but other places of articulation are possible. Velar examples would be *len*[k]*th*, *stren*[k]*th*, *youn*[k]*ster*, *gan*[k]*ster*. Bilabial examples would be *some*[p]*thing* and *Sam*[p]*son and Delilah*. Before a postalveolar fricative, an epenthetic stop creates the affricate [tʃ], e.g. *finan*[tʃ]*al*. (A dental example would be the word *epen*[t̪]*thesis* itself.)

Some speakers have categorical epenthesis, so their words never contain a nasal directly followed by a voiceless fricative, unless a stressed vowel follows. Categorical epenthesis wasn't characteristic of RP, but today many SSB speakers have this feature.

For such speakers, quite a few contrasts are lost. Aside from *prince-prints*, common ones are *mince-mints*, *sense-cents*, *dense-dents*, *tense-tents* and *chance-chants*. A larger group of pairs have the unstressed endings *-ence/-ance* and *-ents/-ants*; a list is given below.

Many speakers have not lost these contrasts, and many others use epenthesis variably. For the learner, it's worth being aware of epenthesis, but not yet important to adopt it.

Pairs with *-ence/-ance* and *-ents/ants*

accidence-accidents, adherence-adherents, adolescence-adolescents, antecedence-antecedents, attendance-attendants, consonance-consonants, continence-continents, convalescence-convalescents, decadence-decadents, deterence-deterents, deviance-deviants, dissidence-dissidents, effluence-effluents, entrance-entrants, equivalence-equivalents, gradience-gradients, incidence-indicents, independence-independents, innocence-innocents, insurgence-insurgents, patience-patients, penance-pennants, penitence-penitents, precedence-precedents, presence-presents, residence-residents, sibilance-sibilants, succulence-succulents, Torrance-torrents, transience-transients, variance-variants.

Chapter 18

Syllabic Consonants: A *little* Less *certain*

In Brief In RP, syllabic /l/ and /n/ were very common, e.g. *little* [ˈlɪtl̩], *certain* [ˈsə:tn̩]. Many speakers today pronounce such syllables with normally released /t/ and /d/ followed by a weak vowel, e.g. *little* ˈlɪtəl, *certain* ˈsə:tən.

In RP, hundreds of words had weak syllables containing not a vowel, but syllabic /l/ and /n/, i.e. [l̩] and [n̩]. These syllabic consonants were preceded directly by a consonant, often the alveolar plosives /t/ or /d/. Examples would be *little* [ˈlɪtl̩] and *certain* [ˈsə:tn̩].

If syllabic /l/ and /n/ are preceded by an alveolar plosive, the plosive is not released at the alveolar ridge in the normal way, as in *two* or *do*. In the case of syllabic /l/, as in *little* [ˈlɪtl̩] and *middle* [ˈmɪdl̩], the plosive is released laterally, by lowering the sides of the tongue. In the case of syllabic /n/, as in *certain* [ˈsə:tn̩] and *or*[dn̩]*ary,* the plosive is released nasally, by lowering the soft palate at the back of the mouth, allowing airflow through the nose.

Many speakers still use such syllabic consonants. But pronunciations without syllabic consonants are increasingly heard, especially among younger speakers. In such pronunciations, a normally-released plosive is

© The Author(s) 2019
G. Lindsey, *English After RP*, https://doi.org/10.1007/978-3-030-04357-5_19

followed by schwa /ə/, e.g. *little* ˈlɪtəl, *certain* ˈsɜːtən, or by weak KIT, e.g. *ordinary* ˈoːdɪnrɪj.

The change is more advanced in some words than others. *Italy* and *important,* for example, are very widely heard with [tə]. The reintroduction of vowels into such words can be seen as one of the ways in which pronunciation has been brought more into line with spelling; see Chap. 1.

Chapter 19

Glottal Stops, Part 1

In Brief The glottal stop [ʔ] was not characteristic of RP, but is very common today as a form of /t/, being entirely standard before consonants, e.g. *foo_t_ball*, *Grea_t_ Britain*.

In the remaining chapters of this section on consonants, we'll look at pronunciation features which during the RP era were famously characteristic of working class London speech, or 'Cockney'. These features were stigmatized to varying degrees, and RP speakers generally avoided them; but they can all be heard from the more middle-class speakers of SSB today. We'll look at them in decreasing order of their integration into 'standard' speech.

In a glottal stop [ʔ], the vocal cords are held together, cutting off the airstream from the lungs. The glottal stop was not characteristic of RP, but it's now a very common syllable-final form of /t/. Today it's entirely standard to replace syllable-final [t] with [ʔ] before a consonant, whether the consonant is in the same word or not.

(a) **Word-internal before a consonant:**

depar[ʔ]ment, fi[ʔ]ness, foo[ʔ]ball, ne[ʔ]work, ou[ʔ]door, par[ʔ]ner, pla[ʔ]form, Sco[ʔ]land, sligh[ʔ]ly, sta[ʔ]ment, trea[ʔ]ment

© The Author(s) 2019
G. Lindsey, *English After RP*, https://doi.org/10.1007/978-3-030-04357-5_20

(b) **Word-final before a consonant:**

> *abou*[ʔ]*now, a lo*[ʔ]*more, a*[ʔ]*least, ge*[ʔ]*ready, Grea*[ʔ]*Britain,
> ou*[ʔ]*there, par*[ʔ]*time, spor*[ʔ]*lover, suppor*[ʔ]*network, tha*[ʔ]*one,
> wha*[ʔ]*for*

(Using a glottal stop simultaneously with [t], or 'glottal reinforcement', is a common alternative; before a consonant, glottal replacement and glottal reinforcement may be hard to distinguish.)

Many speakers in Britain also use glottal replacement before a vowel. However, this is widely perceived as less standard, particularly when it occurs within a word. Visitors to Britain are likely to hear pronunciations like the following, but it's very unlikely that they would be used by a newsreader:

(c) **Word-internal before a vowel:**

> *ar*[ʔ]*icle, be*[ʔ]*er, Bri*[ʔ]*ish, capi*[ʔ]*al, ci*[ʔ]*y, digi*[ʔ]*al, la*[ʔ]*est,
> limi*[ʔ]*ed, pho*[ʔ]*o, quali*[ʔ]*y, par*[ʔ]*ty, Twi*[ʔ]*er, uni*[ʔ]*ed, universi*[ʔ]*y,
> wa*[ʔ]*er*

Note that such word-internal glottal replacement only happens before an unstressed vowel. This restriction does not apply when the following vowel is in the next word:

(d) **Word-final before a vowel:**

> *abou*[ʔ]*eight, a lo*[ʔ]*of, a*[ʔ]*any price, ge*[ʔ]*out, Grea*[ʔ]*Expectations,
> ou*[ʔ]*of order, par*[ʔ]*exchange, suppor*[ʔ]*each other, tha*[ʔ]*is, wha*[ʔ]*else*

Glottal replacement of type d. is increasingly common in SSB. It may be considered less standard than types a. and b., but it's decidedly less stigmatized than type c. The same is true of glottal replacement at the end of a phrase, e.g. *I don't like tha*[ʔ].

For learners of English from many language backgrounds, it's worth learning glottal replacement before a consonant (types a. and b.). Spanish speakers, for example, readily lose /t/ altogether in this context, and the glottal stop is a more native-like way of preserving the consonant than exploding the [t] forcefully. Before a vowel, it's better to preserve the [t] with word-linking, e.g. *can't agree* ˈkɑːntəˈɡrɪj.

/t/-voicing

An alternative to the glottal replacement of /t/ is /t/-voicing: that is, using [d] or the tap [ɾ] which is familiar in North American pronunciation.

This is not a general phenomenon in SSB, but is very common in some words like *British* and *pretty* (as in *pretty much*), and at the end of short words like *at, but, get, got, it, lot, not, put, that, what,* when a vowel follows immediately. Examples:

a[d]*any price, ge*[d]*out, a lo*[d]*of, no*[d]*only, bu*[d]*also, pu*[d]*i*[d]*away, tha*[d]*alone, wha*[d]*else*

Chapter 20

Is /l/ Following /r/?

In Brief In Southern Britain, /r/ is only pronounced when a vowel follows. This is also true of /l/ for many speakers, who use a vocalic sound instead when no vowel follows. In the RP era this was a stigmatized 'Cockney' feature, but it's now more common and accepted.

In Southern Britain, /r/ is only pronounced when a vowel sound immediately follows. So /r/ is pronounced in *three* and *very* and *four o'clock,* but not in *bored* or *early* or *fourteen* (the *e* in *bored* is silent). This is also true of the Southern Hemisphere Englishes. It's not true, however, in Scotland, Ireland and North America, where the historic, written *r* survives in pronunciation. Such accents are called 'rhotic', while restricted-/r/ accents like those of Southern Britain are called 'non-rhotic'. The loss of /r/ happened in the London area over two centuries ago, and was established in time for it to be a feature of the accent which came to be known as RP (see Introduction).

The consonants /r/ and /l/ have much in common, and together are known as the 'liquids'. Some languages, and some varieties of English, restrict the occurrence of /l/ in much the same way that non-rhotic accents restrict the occurrence of /r/. This happens through '/l/-vocalization': the replacement of /l/ by a more vowel-like sound.

G. Lindsey, *English After RP*, https://doi.org/10.1007/978-3-030-04357-5_21

Cockney, the traditional working class accent of London, had extensive /l/-vocalization. So Cockneys pronounced /l/ before a vowel, in e.g. *London, please* and *belly,* but elsewhere vocalized it to a sound more like [ʊ] or [w], e.g. *film* [fɪʊm] or [fɪwm], *bell* [beʊ] or [bew].

RP did not go so far as to vocalize /l/, but rather gave it a 'dark' pronunciation [ɫ], with the body of the tongue retracted, in the contexts where Cockney vocalized it: *film* [fɪɫm], *bell* [beɫ].

Today, /l/-vocalization is heard not only in the broad accent of the London area, but also from many individuals whose speech is otherwise standard; a prominent example is the celebrity politician Boris Johnson. This has led some to speculate that /l/ will become as generally restricted in SSB as /r/ is, i.e. pronounced only before a vowel.

However, a majority of the more visible and influential SSB speakers – TV presenters, actors, politicians, etc. – retain /l/ in all contexts, with the dark form [ɫ] when no vowel follows. And many of those who don't use /l/-vocalization perceive extensive use of it as a regionally or socially specific feature.

The best advice for learners aiming at a British accent is, if possible, to learn and practise the two forms of /l/, clear before a vowel and dark elsewhere. For learners who find syllable-final /l/ very challenging, including many Japanese and Chinese speakers, a vocalized form like [ʊ] or [o] is less likely to be perceived as wrong than it was in the days of RP.

Chapter 21

G-dropping and H-dropping

In Brief Pronouncing *-ing* as /ɪn/ and dropping /h/ from stressed sylla-bles were both stigmatized in the RP era. Today neither is considered standard, but /ɪn/ for *-ing* is used by numerous prominent people and can be heard in TV news.

Some traditional features of popular London speech were heavily stig-matized in the RP era. Two of these were 'G-dropping' and 'H-dropping'. Although they'd both been features of aristocratic speech in earlier times, they were disallowed in twentieth century RP.

'G-dropping' refers to the pronunciation of the weak ending *-ing* as /ɪn/ rather than /ɪŋ/. In vernacular speech, /ɪn/ for *-ing* is common, prob-ably more so in America. In popular music, it's absolutely normal to sing *-ing* as /ɪn/, and the spelling *-in'* is common, e.g. Bob Dylan's *Blowin' in the Wind*.

However, /ɪn/ for *-ing* is much rarer in more formal settings and is widely considered incorrect. Nonetheless it's less stigmatized than it was, and it can be heard from numerous people in public life, such as London Mayor Sadiq Khan, and from some people in TV news.

© The Author(s) 2019
G. Lindsey, *English After RP*, https://doi.org/10.1007/978-3-030-04357-5_22

For learners aiming at a British accent, it's worth practising the ending *-ing* as /ɪŋ/; but for those who find this very challenging, the /ɪn/ pronunciation isn't as stigmatized as it was.

'H-dropping' refers to the loss of /h/ from stressed syllables. It can be indicated in writing with an apostrophe, e.g. *Harry* as *'Arry*, *hello* as *'ello*, *horrible* as *'orrible*. This sometimes occurs in the more informal speech of speakers who usually retain /h/, e.g. *I 'aven't done it yet*. But the consistent loss of /h/ from stressed syllables, though common in various British accents, cannot be considered a feature of SSB. Note that H-dropping is less common in today's London vernacular than it was in traditional Cockney, since it's absent from the 'Multicultural London English' now used by many young people.

By contrast, loss of /h/ is widespread and standard when weak words like *he*, *him*, *his*, *her* and auxiliary *have* are connected to a preceding word. For example, *Give him* [gɪvɪm] *my regards*, *When has* [wɛnəz] *it got to be done by?*

Chapter 22

Fings to Come?

In Brief In recent years, the replacement of /θ/ and /ð/ with /f/, /v/ and /d/ has become common among younger speakers across Britain, and it may occasionally be heard from television presenters. It's not yet considered a standard feature, but this may change in future.

In this chapter, we look at a development that has recently become far more widespread than it was, though it's not become an established feature of SSB. This is the replacement of the 'th' sounds with other pronunciations, widely known as TH-fronting.

The English 'th' sounds are dental fricatives, made with the tip of the tongue at or near the upper teeth. Voiceless /θ/ occurs in *thin*, *author* and *breath*; voiced /ð/ occurs in *then*, *other* and *breathe*. These sounds are relatively rare in the world's languages, and they're among the last sounds to be acquired by native-speaking children. This suggests that they're intrinsically rather tricky articulations. Most non-natives find them challenging.

In several native varieties of English, these sounds are avoided some or all of the time. Cockney, the traditional working class accent of London, was notable for replacing word-initial /ð/ with /d/ and otherwise replacing

© The Author(s) 2019
G. Lindsey, *English After RP*, https://doi.org/10.1007/978-3-030-04357-5_23

/θ/ with /f/ and /ð/ with /v/. In Cockney, *this* could be /dɪs/, *think* could be /fɪŋk/, and *other* could be /ˈʌvə/.

Many speakers of such varieties make these changes in some words, but not in others, so that they haven't lost /θ/ and /ð/ entirely. For example, some London speakers keep /ð/ in *the* but pronounce *with* as /wɪv/.

RP speakers did not make replacements of this kind. In the RP era, the loss of the 'th' sounds was restricted to broad lower-class speech in London and a few other locations, and was heavily stigmatized. But for some time now, it's been noticed that TH-fronting is becoming considerably more widespread. It can be heard across Britain, from speakers in all educational and socio-economic groups, mainly from the young but also from some in middle age. It's occasionally heard, in some words at least, from television presenters, including some in TV news.

The most common replacements from such speakers are /ð/ > /v/ in frequently used words such as *another, further, other, together, whether, without*. The replacement of /θ/ by /f/ seems to be relatively common in the word *through*.

It's remarkable that this change has spread rapidly both in geographical and social terms. It seems likely that its use will increase, and some pronunciations with replacements of /θ/ and /ð/ may become established as standard. It's even conceivable, in the more distant future, that /θ/ and /ð/ will become endangered sounds in Britain.

Note that native speakers don't generally replace /θ/ and /ð/ with /s/ and /z/; this is perceived as foreign. Learners who find /θ/ and /ð/ very difficult may be better advised to use /f/ and /v/.

Part IV

Stress

Chapter 23

The Love of Alternating Stress

In Brief RP was relatively tolerant of words with sequences of weak syllables, such as *applicable* and *hospitable*, which were stressed on the first syllable. A number of these words are now heard with shifted stress, reducing the number of successive weak syllables.

English has a preference for weaker and stronger syllables to alternate in sequence, which is sometimes called 'alternating stress'. Shakespeare's rhythm strictly regularizes this tendency:

A ˈrose by ˈany ˈother ˈname would ˈsmell as ˈsweet.

Such patterns emerge quite readily from English speakers, like the title of this chapter:

The ˈlove of ˈalterˈnating ˈstress

Of course, normal spoken English often deviates from precise alternating stress. Many words contain adjacent stressed syllables:

ˌthirˈteen   ˈnewsˌpaper   the ˌU.ˈK.

© The Author(s) 2019
G. Lindsey, *English After RP*, https://doi.org/10.1007/978-3-030-04357-5_24

And many words contain adjacent weak syllables:

ˈcustomer   deˈvelopment   ˌnevertheˈless

RP was relatively tolerant of words with sequences of weak syllables. Many common words had initial stress followed by three or even four weak syllables in succession, e.g. *applicable* /ˈæplɪkəbəl/ and *disciplinary* /ˈdɪsɪplɪnərɪ/.

In contemporary speech, there are still some common words with three and four weak syllables, including *difficulty, knowledgeable* and *speculatively.* But a number of such words, including *applicable* and *disciplinary,* have decisively shifted the main stress onto their antepenultimate syllables, reducing the sequences of weak syllables to two: **əˈplɪkəbəl** and **ˌdɪsəˈplɪnərɪj**.

Another way of avoiding three successive weak syllables in such words is to eliminate the first of the weak vowels. This has been common since the RP era in words such as *comfortable* /ˈkʌmftəbəl/ and *vegetable* /ˈvedʒtəbəl/, and in words ending -*rable,* such as *considerable* /kənˈsɪdrəbəl/ and *favourable* /ˈfeɪvrəbəl/. In some words, both options can now be heard; for example, *comparable* can be heard both as three-syllable **ˈkɒmprəbəl** and, especially from younger speakers, as four syllables but with the main stress on the second syllable, **kəmˈparəbəl**.

A number of three-syllable words have also shifted in favour of alternating stress. Examples include *communal* and *exquisite,* which RP preferred to give initial stress, with two following weak syllables, whereas the modern preference is for stress on the middle syllable. (On the other hand, *sonorous* has moved in the opposite direction, from medial to initial stress.) Again, an alternative strategy is to lose the first of the weak vowels, common in RP before /l/ or /r/ in words like *chocolate* /ˈtʃɒklət/ and *camera* /ˈkæmrə/, and occurring more recently in words like *diamond* **ˈdajmənd** and *violence* **ˈvajlən(t)s**.

A further change which promotes weak-strong alternation is the strengthening of the ending -*ary,* as in American English, which some SSB speakers now use in words such as *necessary, February, ordinary* and *secretary,* e.g. **ˈnesəserɪj**. (The same applies to the ending -*on* in words such as *aeon, paragon* and *polygon.*) Words ending -*rary* had /rərɪ/ in RP but are now widely heard with loss of the first weak syllable /rə/, e.g. *library* **ˈlajbrɪj**.

Common words which still end in three weak syllables:

- *admirable, charitable, eligible, enviable, inevitable, inexorable, irritable, knowledgeable, manageable, noticeable, practicable, profitable, reputable, serviceable, variable*
- *accuracy, ceremony, difficulty, occupancy, residency*
- *administrative, illustrative*
- *-ly* words, e.g. *fortunately, relatively*

Words exhibiting a shift from initial stress to second-syllable stress:

- *applicable, comparable, controversy, demonstrable, formidable, hospitable, lamentable, transferable*
- *communal, exquisite, omega, quadruple, subsidence*

Words which usually or commonly lose /ə/ in the syllable before -able:

- *comfortable, vegetable*
- *comparable, considerable, decipherable, deliverable, favourable, honourable, inseparable, insuperable, irreparable, memorable, miserable, vulnerable* (usually the first /ɪ/ is lost in three-syllable *vulnerable,* ˈvʌnrəbəl)

Chapter 24

Westward Toward America?

In Brief Many words have earlier stress in America than in Britain. However, this is less true now than it was in RP, as numerous words have changed, or are changing, to earlier stress.

There are many words which have early stress in the preferred American pronunciation and later stress in the preferred British pronunciation. *Donate, inquiry, spectator, urinal,* for example, are stressed on the first syllable in America and on the second in Britain. Some instances are compounds or names, with main stress on the first part in America and on the second part in Britain, e.g. *boy scout, pork chop, Robin Hood, Hong Kong*.

These differences were considerably greater in RP than they are today. That is, many of the relevant items exhibit a 'westward' stress shift, with the early stress patterns preferred in America becoming more common in Britain. Some of these shifts are more established than others: initial stress is now preferred in *ice cream,* except among older speakers; both initial and final stress are widely heard in *weekend*; while initial stress on *Pakistan* is still relatively rare in Britain, but can be heard from younger speakers.

It's likely that exposure to American English has played a role in this leftward shift of stress. But some cases of leftward stress shift don't reflect

© The Author(s) 2019
G. Lindsey, *English After RP*, https://doi.org/10.1007/978-3-030-04357-5_25

American pronunciation; notable examples are *contribute* and *distribute*, which in RP had second-syllable stress as in America, but which are now widely given initial stress in Britain.

In loanwords from French, American English generally has **later** stress than British English. *Ballet, café, massage* and *salon* all have final stress in America and initial stress in Britain. But some French loans have shifted rightwards since RP, to the American pattern: *potpourri* now has final stress in SSB, and *debris* is also heard widely with final stress, especially from younger speakers.

Now widely heard with initial stress, as in American English:

- *Big Mac, cigarette, cottage cheese, co-worker, cream cheese, French fries, furthermore, headquarters, ice cream, magazine, mayonnaise, parmesan, peanut butter, polar bear, princess, salad dressing, shortcut, weekend*
- *to finance, to protest, to transport; research* (noun and verb)

Part V

Connected Speech

Chapter 25

Linking /r/

In Brief RP speakers were encouraged to be spelling-conscious when using linking /r/ between words: if there was no written *r* at the end of the first word, e.g. *vanilla ice,* then a linking /r/ was considered 'intrusive'. Today, unwritten linking /r/ is no longer discouraged, and learners should expect to hear it in Southern British pronunciation.

In the era of RP, it was considered important to distinguish 'linking r' and 'intrusive r'.

'Linking r' refers to the /r/ heard in phrases such as *far away* and *War and Peace*. A word like *far*, when pronounced alone, has no final /r/ in Southern Britain: /fɑː/. However, when a vowel follows, a linking /r/ is typically added: e.g. /fɑːr/*away.*

'Intrusive r' was the name given to a linking /r/ if there was no corresponding *r* in the spelling. Examples would be *vanilla*/r/*ice* and *law* /r/*and order*. In such cases, the /r/ was considered an 'intrusion', and many people condemned it, despite the fact that English pronunciation very frequently diverges from spellings.

Some even claimed that 'intrusive r' was not a feature of RP. However, we have many recordings, going back over 80 years, of RP speakers using unwritten linking /r/, including actors and newsreel narrators.

© The Author(s) 2019
G. Lindsey, *English After RP*, https://doi.org/10.1007/978-3-030-04357-5_26

Clips from such recordings can be heard on my website, at https://www.englishspeechservices.com/blog/linking-r/.

The main change since RP regarding unwritten linking /r/ is that it's no longer condemned; most SSB speakers today make no effort to suppress it. It can be heard in practically every BBC news broadcast, e.g. *America/r/and China, Obama/r/administration. Pizza/r/Express* is the standard pronunciation in England of a well-known restaurant chain, and the TV series *Law and Order* is routinely announced as *Law/r/and Order.*

We can state very simply the rule which inserts linking /r/ before a following vowel. It may be inserted after all vowels except the closing diphthongs: in other words, after NEAR, SQUARE, START, NORTH, NURSE, CURE, and schwa. (The other short vowels never occur before another vowel.)

Three of these vowels occur in words without written *r*. The START vowel, which is also the PALM vowel, occurs on the end of both *spar* and *spa*. The NORTH vowel, which is also the THOUGHT vowel, occurs on the end of both *nor* and *gnaw*. And schwa occurs on the end of both *stellar* and *Stella*. Linking /r/ may be used after all three of these vowels, regardless of whether the spelling has an *r*.

Non-native speakers have typically learned English through the writing system, and pronounce /r/ only when they see it written. Whether or not they learn to use unwritten linking /r/ like natives, they should be prepared to hear it frequently in native speech.

Note that linking /r/ is not the only option when a word ending in one of the seven vowels listed above is followed by another vowel. Alternatively, the words may be separated with a glottal stop; this is the topic of the following chapter.

Examples of unwritten linking /r/

* After schwa
  idea/r/of it, data/r/analysis, Obama/r/administration, Pizza/r/Express, vanilla/r/ice cream

- After PALM
grandma/r/and grandpa, Omaha/r/insurance, Shah/r/of Iran, spa/r/ and massage

- After THOUGHT
law/r/enforcement, I saw/r/everything, gnaw/r/on a bone, thaw/r/it out, draw/r/ing

Chapter 26

Glottal Stops, Part 2

In Brief Glottal stops are sometimes used as a way to begin a word-initial vowel. In RP, this was seen mainly as a way to emphasize the word. Today, initial glottal stops are also quite often used unemphatically, to separate words in connected speech.

In Chap. 19, we looked at the use of the glottal stop in SSB as a replacement for the consonant [t]. Another use of the glottal stop is as a way of beginning a vowel at the start of a word. This is referred to as 'hard attack'.

RP's use of hard attack was described by John Wells in his *Longman Pronunciation Dictionary*: 'In English, hard attack is not customary. But it is sometimes used for special effect, as way of emphasizing the importance of a word.' In other words, hard attack in RP was seen as a property of an individual word, picked out for special emphasis. For example, 'am' in 'I[ʔ]am!'

In contemporary speech, hard attack can still be used to emphasize an important word. But very often it's used not to emphasize a word but to separate words in connected speech.

Without hard attack, the two words in a sequence like *I am* are pronounced in 'close juncture', just like the first two syllables of *diameter*.

© The Author(s) 2019
G. Lindsey, *English After RP*, https://doi.org/10.1007/978-3-030-04357-5_27

| I am | /aɪæm/ | **ɑjam** |
| diameter | /daɪæmɪtə/ | **dɑjamɪtə** |

Hard attack, on the other hand, creates a separating break between the words, **ɑj[ʔ]am**. This can be heard commonly today before words which are not particularly important, including function words, and which are not being emphasized. Here are real examples from TV news:

> the murder[ʔ]of a British couple
> there[ʔ]are[ʔ]already reports

In neither of these examples were the words following the glottal stops given special accentuation. Nonetheless, such non-emphatic use of hard attack is more common before stressed than unstressed vowels, and is often used on the strong rather than weak forms of function words. This suggests that it's related to phonological strength rather than to semantic importance. It's also more common at an intonation phrase boundary, separating phrases rather than being assigned to an individual word. And it's much more common in 'presentational' speech such as newsreading, where speakers are under special pressure to be clear, than in conversation.

For learners, these points suggest that, despite an apparent increase in the use of hard attack, they shouldn't adopt it as a general way of beginning word-initial vowels. Very heavy use of hard attack contributes to the foreignness of an accent, and learners aiming at native-like speech are better advised to practise the linking of words with close juncture. See Chaps. 5 and 25.

Learners are advised to avoid hard attack inside words, e.g. *di*[ʔ]*ameter*. Natives use it only rarely inside words – which further supports the idea that it's being used to separate words rather than to emphasize them.

To and *the*

Three of the most common English words which end in vowels are the preposition *to* and the articles *the* and *a*. These three words generally have schwa /ə/ before consonants. Before vowels, their forms alter: the indefinite article acquires /n/, while *to* and *the* typically change their vowels, becoming /tuː/ **tʉw** and /ðiː/ **ðɪj**. For example:

a dress	ə'drɛs	*an address*	ənə'drɛs
to dress	tə'drɛs	*to address*	tʉwə'drɛs
the dress	ðə'drɛs	*the address*	ðɪjə'drɛs

Many younger speakers of SSB now use schwa before vowels as well as consonants, but with hard attack before a vowel:

to address	tə[ʔ]ə'drɛs
the address	ðə[ʔ]ə'drɛs

(This pattern is more established in America, and perhaps in Scotland, than in SSB.)

In the case of *the*, such speakers sometimes use both hard attack and the vowel change, e.g. **ðɪj[ʔ]ə'drɛs**. Speakers who use *to* and *the* with following hard attack do so quite generally, and not as a way of emphasizing the following word.

Note that this creates a potential ambiguity in SSB, between the definite article *the* pronounced with hard attack before a vowel, [ðəʔ], and the conjunction *that* pronounced weakly as [ðəʔ] with glottal replacement of the final /t/. For example, in the sentence 'She said [ðəʔ]others will be there', [ðəʔ] could be either *the* or *that*.

When *to* and *the* are pronounced with schwa before a vowel, linking /r/ is **never** used. Learners must avoid *to address* *tərə'drɛs, *the address* *ðərə'drɛs.

Chapter 27

Vocal Fry

In Brief In RP, vocal fry (creaky voice) at the end of utterances was a feature of male speech. Today, on the other hand, it's more commonly used by younger females.

Vocal fry is also known as creak or creaky voice. It refers to very low frequency voicing – the vocal cords vibrating far less often per second than in normal voice. Such voicing is often irregular, with successive vocal cord vibrations differing in duration and/or amplitude. The term 'fry' evokes the sound of a bubbling frying pan; the term 'creaky' evokes the sound of an unoiled door hinge.

When I was a student, I was taught that creaky voice was characteristic of male RP speakers. It was often heard in male RP speech at the end of utterances after falling intonation: instead of ending with low-pitched normal voice, such utterances could descend even further, into creak.

A famous example can be heard in the first James Bond film, *Dr. No*, when the hero introduces himself for the first time as 'Bond, James Bond': after the falling intonation on *James*, the second *Bond* is in creaky voice. (Sean Connery's attempt to speak RP was not very successful, but he got this feature right.) And in the Disney animated film *Jungle Book*, the tiger

© The Author(s) 2019
G. Lindsey, *English After RP*, https://doi.org/10.1007/978-3-030-04357-5_28

Shere Khan is voiced by RP-accented George Sanders, whose utterances very frequently have creaky endings.

More recently in Britain, terminal creaky voice has become much less used by older males, but can often be heard in the speech of younger females. The latter phenomenon seems to have arisen first in America, where the term vocal fry is preferred.

As is often the case when new linguistic patterns are noticed, the popular press has given quite a lot of negative and inaccurate attention to the new vocal fry. One misleading idea is that it's due to the singer Britney Spears. However, she uses creak in a very different way, at the beginning of sung phrases; other singers have done this before and since, including males. The complaints seem to be largely sexist and ageist: there were no complaints about creaky voice, as far as I'm aware, when it was a male, RP feature.

Some younger males also use vocal fry, and some speakers use it more extensively in their speech than after falling intonation. It may also be that the perception of increased vocal fry is partly due to an increase in the use of pre-vowel glottal stops (see Chap. 26), since glottal stops in reality are usually short periods of creaky voice.

However, most SSB speakers, even younger females, don't use vocal fry extensively. There's therefore little reason for learners of English to make an effort to adopt it.

A longer discussion of vocal fry, with many audio illustrations, is given in my blog article *Britney, Pitney and vocal fry*: https://www.english-speechservices.com/blog/britney-pitney-and-vocal-fry/

Part VI

Intonation

Intonation can be treated as having three sub-systems:

1. Phrasing, the division of the speech stream into chunks, each of which has a self-contained intonation pattern (sometimes called 'tonality')
2. Accentuation, the positioning within a phrase of pitch-accents, most importantly the last or 'nuclear' pitch-accent (sometimes called 'tonicity')
3. Contour, the choice of high, low, rising or falling patterns (sometimes called 'tone')

Neither phrasing nor accentuation has changed significantly since the RP era. Phrasing is intimately connected with grammatical structure, which tends to change less over time than pronunciation. Accentuation is also quite stable, although the stress patterns of many individual words have changed (see Chaps. 23 and 24). Learners from many language backgrounds must still familiarize themselves with the various ways in which English can place the last pitch-accent early in a phrase, with the result that many English phrases end in accentless content words.

On the other hand, the use of contour has changed quite a lot: aside from vowels, intonation contour is perhaps the feature of RP which sounds most old-fashioned and amusing to native speakers today.

The best-known description of RP intonation is by O'Connor and Arnold (1973), who listed the ten contours (or 'tone groups') which they considered the most common in RP. These included some that are relatively rare today, while some of today's most common contours were not included; and some of their contours, though still common, now have rather different meanings.

Individual changes are discussed below. But one generalization is that RP made greater use of **downstep** than contemporary intonation. Downstep refers to contours with a step down in pitch onto the last, nuclear pitch-accent, so that the nuclear syllable begins at a lower pitch than what precedes. Three of O'Connor & Arnold's ten contours featured downstep: the 'Low Drop', the 'Low Bounce' and the 'Terrace'. While these contours are by no means extinct, their use is now more restricted, and they can even sound 'patronizing' or at least old-fashioned. In general, other contours are more recommendable to today's learners.

Chapter 28

Falls

In Brief A falling pitch is common at the end of intonation phrases, and the fall may be from relatively high or relatively low. Low falls seem to have been more common in RP than they are today, and they may now even have a patronizing connotation.

The first two RP intonation contours which O'Connor & Arnold described were the 'Low Drop' and the 'High Drop'. Both of these feature a final nuclear falling tone, which can be preceded by a high 'head' (the stretch from the first accented syllable up to, but not including, the nuclear syllable). In the High Drop, the nuclear tone is a High Fall: it falls from high to low. In the Low Drop, the nuclear tone is a Low Fall, falling from mid to low; this means there's a step down in pitch from the head to the nuclear syllable. We can call this a downstepped fall.

In the following examples, the nuclear syllable is underlined.

The High Drop (ending in a High Fall):

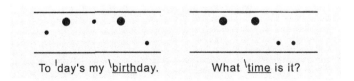

The Low Drop (ending in a downstepped Low Fall):

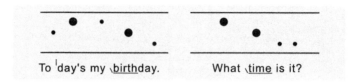

The difference in meaning, according to O'Connor & Arnold, was that the Low Drop was 'weighty' and 'serious', while the High Drop was 'light' and 'airy'. They pointed out that the High Drop was 'very frequently used in everyday conversation.'

O'Connor & Arnold's description is still broadly true. But the downstepped Low Drop is today less common than it was, and the modern learner should see the High Drop as basic and neutral. The High Drop is very common on statements and wh-questions, and is therefore very important to master. The Low Drop, on the other hand, is more marginal and not recommendable as a basic, neutral way of speaking. This advice is important for speakers of the many languages which often use a gradually falling pitch across their utterances, descending to a low fall at the end. It might help to think of English phrases as preferring to end with a climactic high fall rather than a 'dying away' slump.

The Low Drop hasn't vanished, but its uses today are more restricted and marked. The 'weighty' and 'serious' connotation described by O'Connor & Arnold made it a popular contour for Margaret Thatcher. Today the downstep from high pre-nuclear pitch to the low nuclear fall can even sound 'patronizing' or 'haughty' – as RP can in general.

One type of utterance on which downstepped falls are still often used is announcements, on radio and television, in public transport systems, etc. This may be because downstep can have a somewhat 'authoritative' sound – as, again, RP can in general.

If preceded by a high level pitch or a gradually falling pitch (a 'Falling Head'), the Low Fall is relatively calm and formal:

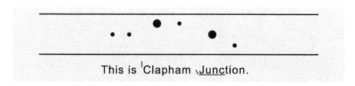

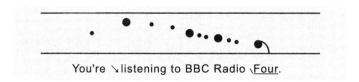

You're ↘listening to BBC Radio ↘Four.

On the other hand, if preceded by a gradually **rising** pitch (a 'Rising Head'), the result is a more excited tone which has become extremely fashionable in less formal announcements.

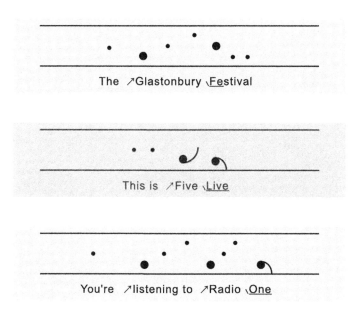

The ↗Glastonbury ↘Festival

This is ↗Five ↘Live

You're ↗listening to ↗Radio ↘One

(BBC Radio Four is aimed at older, more educated listeners; BBC Radio One is a pop-rock station for a younger audience.)

The simplest advice for learners interested in intonation is to acquaint yourself with the downstepped fall, but generally to be wary of using it. (The same advice applies to all downstepping patterns.) The High Fall tone is more recommendable for day-to-day use.

Chapter 29

Yes-No Questions

In Brief It was very common in RP to ask yes-no questions with the downstepped Low Rise, but this can now sound old-fashioned or even patronizing.

One of the most significant changes in intonation since RP is in yes-no questions, i.e. questions which can be answered 'yes' or 'no'. O'Connor and Arnold (1973) stated that 'by far the most common way of asking yes-no questions' was with the pattern they called the 'Low Bounce'. In this pattern, high pre-nuclear pitch is followed by a marked step down onto a nuclear Low Rise. Here is one of O'Connor & Arnold's examples:

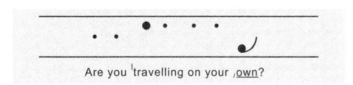

Are you 'travelling on your ˏown?

This pattern can certainly be heard today, but its meaning is more marked and less neutral than it was in RP. It may show considerable surprise; or it may signal that the speaker is talking 'down' to the hearer.

G. Lindsey, *English After RP*, https://doi.org/10.1007/978-3-030-04357-5_30

Adults might use it when asking small children a question. The example above might perhaps be used by an adult who finds a small child travelling alone.

In SSB today, a more neutral and common way of asking yes-no questions is with a contour that O'Connor & Arnold didn't include among their ten basic patterns. This contour begins, like the Low Bounce, with high level pre-nuclear pitch, but it ends in the **Fall-Rise** nuclear tone rather than the Low Rise. This gives us a more straightforwardly polite yes-no question, suitable for any addressee:

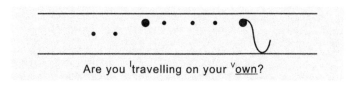

Are you ˈtravelling on your ᵛ<u>own</u>?

The Fall-Rise is very common in SSB, and is discussed further in the next chapter. The learner aiming at an SSB accent should definitely practise it. Downstepped nuclear tones, on the other hand, should be treated with caution.

Americans don't use the Fall-Rise so much on yes-no questions. They're far more likely to use a plain rise, usually without a big step down in pitch from the preceding syllable:

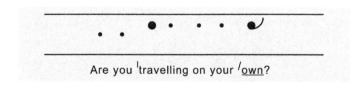

Are you ˈtravelling on your ᐟ<u>own</u>?

This contour, ending in a High Rise tone, is also common in SSB, existing alongside the Fall-Rise pattern. Additionally, it's often heard now on statements, in many parts of the English-speaking world. This 'Uptalk' is discussed in Chap. 31.

Chapter 30

Continuation Patterns

In Brief The Low Rise, Fall-Rise and Mid-Level nuclear tones can all signal non-finality. In RP, the Mid-Level was frequently preceded by higher pitch, but today such downstep is less common and can sound old-fashioned.

As discussed in the previous chapter, the downstepped Low Rise (O'Connor & Arnold's 'Low Bounce') can no longer be seen as the basic pattern for yes-no questions, as it was in RP. But this doesn't mean that the Low Rise nuclear tone has fallen out of use.

The Low Rise is still commonly used on lists – except for the closing item, which has a Fall:

| You'll need /flour | an /egg | /milk | and a pinch of \salt. |

(The pitch of syllables before the Low Rise is usually mid or low.)

The Low Rise is most appropriate in **planned** lists, when the speaker wants to show that they have the whole list already in mind. A television chef might use the intonation in the above example, knowing the whole list in advance.

A different but very common kind of list is **un**planned, when the speaker is adding items to the list spontaneously. If someone is asked whether they need anything from the supermarket, they might reply:

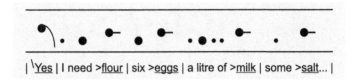

| ˅Yes | I need >flour | six >eggs | a litre of >milk | some >salt... |

This is the Mid-Level nuclear tone. It was also used in RP, but, as described by O'Connor & Arnold, it was generally preceded by the high level head. That combination, which they called the 'Terrace', is another example of the down-step onto the nuclear syllable which was common of RP intonation, but which can now sound old-fashioned or even patronizing. In contemporary intonation, the Mid-Level is more commonly preceded by low pre-nuclear pitch, as shown in the example above (a combination which O'Connor & Arnold didn't include among their ten basic RP patterns).

The non-final items on lists can be seen as just a special case of non-final phrases in general. These are frequently marked by the Low Rise, or the Mid-Level, or the Fall-Rise. So we can say that these three tones are very often used as **continuation patterns**. Any of them can be used to show that you haven't reached your main point yet.

The Fall-Rise is common on the subjects of sentences (other than pronouns), for example in news reporting:

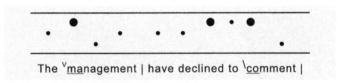

The ˅management | have declined to ˋcomment |

Note that the contemporary Fall-Rise nuclear tone is often not fully realized. Instead of the full high-low-mid pattern, the low pitch may be skipped, so that we hear simply high-mid:

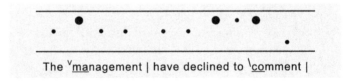

The ˅management | have declined to ˋcomment |

This has been called a 'stylized' Fall-Rise. In natural running speech it can sometimes be tricky to distinguish it from the High Fall.

Chapter 31

Uptalk

In Brief In RP, high rising intonation typically turned a statement into a yes-no question. In recent decades, such intonation has become increasingly used on conversational statements, as way to check that the hearer is following; this is widely known as 'Uptalk'.

In recent decades, one intonational development has attracted more attention than any other. This is 'Uptalk' or the 'High Rising Terminal'. It's not a new contour, but rather a new use of an existing one. O'Connor & Arnold called it the 'High Bounce' pattern, ending in a High Rise nuclear tone.

In RP, if used on a statement, this pattern generally turned it into a yes-no question, as a high rising pitch does in many other languages. For example

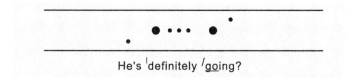

He's ˈdefinitely /g͟oing?

would have much the same meaning as 'Is he definitely going?'

G. Lindsey, *English After RP*, https://doi.org/10.1007/978-3-030-04357-5_32

The contour may still be used in this way, but it also occurs very commonly in a new usage, simply to request acknowledgment that the hearer has understood a **statement**. It's this usage which is known as Uptalk.

Uptalk is similar in function to certain final tags which some speakers use, such as *okay?* or *yeah?* or *right?* Such speakers might say:

> You need to fill out this form, okay?
> We went to that new restaurant, yeah?

The final tag has the effect of seeking some sign from the hearer that the statement is understood. Uptalk achieves this same effect without a tag:

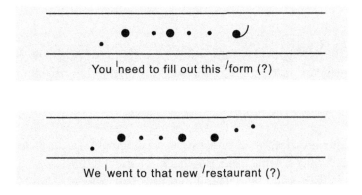

You 'need to fill out this /form (?)

We 'went to that new /restaurant (?)

This is why Uptalk is only used when a hearer is present. It's not used in newsreading, radio talks or public announcements. In classroom lectures, it's not heard as commonly as it is in conversation, but I've heard at least one SSB-speaking professor make use of Uptalk while teaching. The effect is to encourage the students to show, for example by nodding, that they've grasped a particular point.

Use of Uptalk is widespread across the English-speaking world today. It's perhaps most common in Australia, but is also heavily used in America and by many in Britain, though not typically by older British speakers. Uptalk has been discussed a lot in the press, often in negative terms by writers who fail to grasp its function and who underestimate how well established it actually is in conversational speech. I also hear it quite often from young non-native speakers, who either have picked it up by ear (as it's hardly ever taught) or perhaps use it in their native languages too.

Mini Dictionary

This Mini Dictionary lists a number of words which may be widely heard in SSB today with pronunciations differing from those that were preferred in RP.

Most of the words in the Mini Dictionary are very common. The majority of them illustrate the changes discussed in the preceding chapters, so that other words not listed here will share the same feature. The Mini Dictionary makes no claim to completeness.

For each word, a newer and an older pronunciation are given. The notes in each entry indicate whether the newer pronunciation has largely replaced the older one as the preferred pronunciation, or is a widespread alternative to it. In many cases, as mentioned in the notes, the newer pronunciation is more popular with younger speakers, and so may in time come to predominate.

Where possible, the changed feature is highlighted transcriptionally with traditional symbols between slanting brackets, leaving the rest of the word in normal spelling. Additionally, each word is transcribed in full with modern symbols.

© The Author(s) 2019
G. Lindsey, *English After RP*, https://doi.org/10.1007/978-3-030-04357-5

The preference polls conducted some years ago by John Wells for his *Longman Pronunciation Dictionary* have been valuable in compiling the Mini Dictionary. These polls recorded the views of native speakers, young and old, regarding the pronunciation of a range of words. The website YouGlish, at youglish.com, has been very useful in estimating the popularity of common words' variant pronunciations in actual use today.

aeon

Newer: /ˈiːɒn/ **ˈɪjɔn**
Older: /ˈiːən/

In RP, the preferred pronunciation of this word had a weak second syllable containing schwa /ə/. Today the preferred pronunciation has instead the strong LOT vowel. This change brings the word into line with the American pronunciation. (The word may also be heard in both America and Britain with an initial FACE vowel, /ˈeɪɒn/ **ˈɛjɔn**.) See also *paragon, pentagon, polygon* and Chap. 2.

applicable

Newer: /əˈplɪ/cable **əˈplɪkəbəl**
Older: /ˈæplɪ/cable

In RP, the preferred pronunciation of this word had initial stress followed by three weak syllables. Today this has been almost completely replaced by a pronunciation with stress on the second syllable. See also *communal, comparable, demonstrable, disciplinary, exquisite, formidable, omega, quadruple, subsidence,* and Chap. 23.

arbitrarily

Newer: /ˌɑːbəˈtrerəliː/ **ˌɑːbəˈtrɛrəlɪj**
Older: /ˈɑːbɪtrərɪlɪ/

In RP, the preferred pronunciation of this word had initial stress followed by four successive weak syllables. Today the preferred pronunciation has primary stress on the antepenultimate syllable, which now contains the strong DRESS vowel, as in America. See also *necessarily, primarily, temporarily, voluntarily* and Chaps. 2 and 23. The second and fourth vowels may now be KIT or schwa; see Chap. 10.

arbitrary

Newer: /ˈɑːbətriː/ **ˈɑːbətrɪj**
Older: /ˈɑːbɪtrərɪ/

In RP, the preferred pronunciation of this word ended in three weak syllables. Today it's mostly heard as a three-syllable word, avoiding two successive /r/ consonants. See also *library* and Chap. 23. The second vowel may now be KIT or schwa; see Chap. 10.

Asia

Newer: A/ʒə/ ˈɛjʒə
Older: A/ʃə/

The traditional RP pronunciation of this word contained the voiceless fricative /ʃ/. A pronunciation with /ʒ/ became popular some time ago and can now be considered to have replaced the older one. This change brings *Asia* into line with 'si' words like *occasion, invasion* and *persuasion*, and with the American pronunciation. See also *aversion, excursion, version*, and Chap. 2.

assault

Newer: ass/ɒ/lt əˈsɔlt
Older: ass/ɔː/lt

In RP, the preferred pronunciation of this word had the long THOUGHT vowel /ɔː/. Many words in which this vowel was followed by /l/ plus another consonant (particularly /t/ or /s/) are increasingly pronounced with the short LOT vowel. This change is probably not yet as established as it is in the word *salt*; see also *cauldron, false, halt, salt*, and Chap. 7. (Many speakers vocalize the /l/; see Chap. 20.)

ate

Newer: /eɪt/ ɛjt
Older: /et/

In RP, the preferred pronunciation of this word had the short DRESS vowel. Today, the FACE diphthong is preferred, as in *date, late* and *rate*. This change has brought the pronunciation into line with both the spelling and the American pronunciation. See *bedroom, -day, forbade, forehead, handkerchief, hurricane, mayor, mosquito, mushroom, nephew, newspaper, often, portrait*, and Chaps. 1 and 2.

aversion

Newer: aver/ʒən/ əˈvəːʒən
Older: aver/ʃən/

The RP pronunciation of this word contained the voiceless fricative /ʃ/. In recent decades, a pronunciation with /ʒ/ has risen in popularity and is now probably the preferred pronunciation among younger speakers. This change brings the word into line with the American pronunciation. See also *Asia, excursion, version*, and Chap. 2.

bath

Newer: /bɑːθ/ or /bæθ/ **bɑːθ** or **baθ**
RP: /bɑːθ/

Today, as in the RP era, this word is pronounced with the long PALM vowel in the south of England, while the short TRAP vowel is used both in the north of England and in North America. But in the RP era, only the southern pronunciation was considered standard. Today both can be considered standard. See *graph*, and Chap. 11.

bedroom

Newer: bedr/uː/m **ˈbɛdrʉwm**
Older: bedr/ʊ/m

In RP, the preferred pronunciation of this word had a weak FOOT vowel /ʊ/ in the second syllable. Today the preferred pronunciation has the long GOOSE vowel. This brings the word into line with the preferred pronunciation of *room*, and with the most common pronunciation of the spelling 'oo'. See *ate, -day, forbade, forehead, handkerchief, hurricane, mayor, mosquito, mushroom, nephew, newspaper, often, portrait* and Chap. 1. Many younger speakers have /dʒr/ in place of /dr/, giving **ˈbɛdʒrʉwm**; see Chap. 16.

Brexit

See *exit*.

cauldron

Newer: c/ɒ/ldron **ˈkɔldrən**
Older: c/ɔː/ldron

In RP, the preferred pronunciation of this word had the long THOUGHT vowel. Many words in which this vowel was followed by /l/ plus another consonant (particularly /t/ or /s/) are increasingly pronounced with the short LOT vowel. In some common words like *salt*, LOT is now preferred; in rarer words like *cauldron*, THOUGHT is still more common. See also *assault, false, halt, salt* and Chap. 7. Another possibility is /l/ vocalization; see Chap. 20. Many younger speakers have /dʒr/ in place of /dr/, giving ˈkɔldʒrən; see Chap. 16.

cigarette

Newer: ˈcigarette ˈsɪgərɛt
Older: ˌcigaˈrette

In RP, the preferred pronunciation of this word had main stress on the final syllable. Today, a pronunciation with stress on the first syllable is widely heard, and may be the preferred pronunciation among younger speakers. This change brings the word into line with the preferred American pronunciation. See *co-worker, cream cheese, ice cream, finance, princess, protest, research, transport* and Chaps. 2 and 24.

communal

Newer: /kəˈmjuːnəl/ kəˈmjʉwnəl
Older: /ˈkɒmjʊnəl/

In RP, the preferred pronunciation of this word was stressed on the first syllable. Today, the preferred pronunciation is stressed on the second syllable. See also *applicable, comparable, demonstrable, disciplinary, exquisite, formidable, omega, quadruple, subsidence,* and Chap. 23.

comparable

Newer: /kəmˈpærəbəl/ kəmˈparəbəl or ˈkɒmprəbəl
Older: /ˈkɒmpərəbəl/

In RP, the preferred pronunciation of this word was stressed on the first syllable. Today it's increasingly heard with stress on the second syllable. The initial-stressed version is still common, but generally with the second vowel elided. See *applicable, communal, demonstrable, disciplinary, exquisite, formidable, omega, quadruple, subsidence* and Chap. 23.

contribute

Newer: ˈcontribute ˈkɒntrɪbjʉwt
Older: conˈtribute

In RP, the preferred pronunciation of this word had stress on the second syllable, with a weak first syllable, /kənˈtrɪbjuːt/. This is still common, but a pronunciation with initial stress is also widely heard, particularly among younger speakers. This differs from the preferred American pronunciation; see also *controversy, distribute* and Chap. 24.

controversy

Newer: con'troversy **kən'trɒvəsɪj**
Older: 'controversy

In RP, the preferred pronunciation of this word had stress on the first syllable, and could be followed by three weak syllables, /'kɒntrəvəsɪ/. The modern preference, on the other hand, is to put the main stress on the second syllable, usually with a weak first syllable. This differs from the preferred American pronunciation; see *contribute, distribute* and Chaps. 23 and 24.

cool

Newer: /kɔːl/ **koːl**
Older: /kuːl/

In RP, the preferred pronunciation of this word had the back GOOSE vowel, /uː/. The GOOSE vowel is now generally central, except that it's backed before a dark /l/, as in *cool*. For a number of younger speakers, this back vowel is merged with the modern THOUGHT vowel [oː], merging *cool* with *call*. See also *pool, school, you'll* and Chap. 6.

co-worker

Newer: 'co-ˌworker **'kəwˌwəːkə**
Older: ˌco-'worker

This word wasn't widely used in the RP era, *colleague* being the established term; but *co-* formations generally had the main stress after the prefix, e.g. ˌco-di'rector. However, following American usage, *co-worker* has now become common in Britain, with initial stress. The same applies to *co-pilot*. See also *cigarette, cream cheese, finance, ice cream, princess, protest, research, transport*, and Chaps. 2 and 24.

cream cheese

Newer: 'cream ˌcheese **'krɪjm ˌtʃɪjz**
Older: ˌcream 'cheese

In RP, the main stress on this compound noun belonged to the word *cheese*. A common alternative pronunciation in Britain today, especially among younger speakers, has the main stress on *cream*, as is preferred in America. See also *cigarette, co-worker, ice cream, princess, protest, research, transport,* and Chaps. 2 and 24.

crescent

Newer: cre/z/ent **ˈkrɛzənt**
Older: cre/s/ent

In RP, the preferred pronunciation of this word contained a voiceless /s/. Today the preferred pronunciation contains voiced /z/, although the /s/ pronunciation is still quite widely heard. Americans prefer /s/. See also *exit, mausoleum, newspaper* and *transit.*

-day

Newer: /deɪ/ **dɛj**
Older: /dɪ/

In RP, the preferred pronunciations of *Monday, Tuesday* and the other days of the week ended in the weak KIT vowel, e.g. *Monday* /ˈmʌndɪ/. Today the preferred pronunciations end in the FACE vowel, e.g. **ˈmʌndɛj**. This brings these words into line with the pronunciation of the independent word *day*. See *ate, bedroom, forbade, forehead, handkerchief, hurricane, mayor, mosquito, mushroom, nephew, newspaper, often, portrait,* and Chap. 1.

debris

Newer: /dəˈbriː/ **dəˈbrɪj** or **ˈdɛbrɪj**
Older: /ˈdeɪbriː/

In RP, the preferred pronunciation of this loanword from French was stressed on the first syllable and contained the FACE vowel in the first syllable. Today the word is commonly stressed on the second syllable, with schwa /ə/ in the first syllable, as in the American pronunciation. Also widely heard in SSB is an initial-stressed pronunciation with the DRESS vowel in the first syllable. See also *potpourri* and Chap. 2.

debut

Newer: /ˈdeɪbjuː/ **ˈdɛjbjʉw**
Older: /ˈdeɪbuː/

The preferred RP pronunciation of this word for most of the twentieth century lacked a glide after the /b/. In recent decades, a pronunciation with /bj/ has become firmly established, and the glide-less version is now decidedly old-fashioned. Today, as in RP, the first syllable may be heard less commonly with the short DRESS vowel. Americans prefer to stress the word on the final syllable, as is typical in loans from French.

delirious

Newer: **dəˈlɪːrɪjəs**
Older: /dɪˈlɪrɪəs/

In RP, the preferred pronunciation of this word had the short KIT vowel in the stressed syllable. Today, the preferred pronunciation has a long vowel in this syllable. For most speakers this is the contemporary NEAR vowel, which before /r/ is [ɪː]. Others may use the FLEECE vowel. See Chap. 13. In the weak prefix *de-*, where RP preferred /ɪ/, many speakers now have schwa, while some others use FLEECE; see Chap. 10. The RP-era transcription /ɪə/ was ambiguous, since it could stand for a single centring diphthong or for a two-syllable sequence of /ɪ/ plus /ə/. The modern pronunciation is disyllabic, with a tense vowel before schwa; /ɪ/ is no longer permitted before a vowel. See *mausoleum*, *various* and Chap. 8.

demonstrable

Newer: deˈmonstrable **dəˈmɔnstrəbəl**
Older: ˈdemonstrable

In RP, the preferred pronunciation of this word had initial stress followed by three weak syllables, /ˈdemənstrəbəl/. Today this has been almost completely replaced by a pronunciation with stress on the second syllable. See also *applicable, comparable, communal, disciplinary, exquisite, formidable, omega, quadruple, subsidence* and Chap. 23. (In the weak prefix *de-*, where RP preferred /ɪ/, many speakers have schwa, while some others now use FLEECE; see Chap. 10.)

diamond

Newer: /ˈdaɪmənd/ **ˈdɑjmənd**
Older: /ˈdaɪəmənd/

In RP, this word was pronounced with three syllables, though this could be smoothed to [ˈdaəmənd] (see Chap. 12). A three-syllable pronunciation is still widely used, but the word is increasingly heard as two syllables, without the middle schwa. See also *violence* and Chap. 23.

disciplinary
Newer: ˌdisciˈplinary ˌdɪsəˈplɪnərɪj
Older: ˈdisciplinary

In RP, the preferred pronunciation of this word had initial stress followed by four weak syllables, /ˈdɪsɪplɪnərɪ/. Today the preferred pronunciation has the main stress on the third syllable, and a secondary stress on the first. See also *applicable, comparable, communal, demonstrable, exquisite, formidable, omega, quadruple, subsidence* and Chap. 23.

dissect
Newer: d/aɪ/ssect **dɑjˈsɛkt**
Older: d/ɪ/ssect

The preferred pronunciation of this word during the RP era had the short KIT vowel in the first syllable. This began to be displaced some time ago by the pronunciation with the PRICE diphthong, which is now overwhelmingly preferred.

distribute
Newer: ˈdistribute **ˈdɪstrɪbjʉwt**
Older: disˈtribute

In RP, the preferred pronunciation of this word had stress on the second syllable, /dɪsˈtrɪbjuːt/ or /dɪˈstrɪbjuːt/. The later is still common, but a pronunciation with initial stress is also widely heard, particularly among younger speakers. This differs from the preferred American pronunciation; see also *contribute, controversy* and Chap. 24.

drive
Newer: /dʒ/rive **dʒrɑjv**
Older: /d/rive

In RP, /tr/ and /dr/ clusters were pronounced as postalveolar affricates, but at a phonemic level began with /t/ and /d/. Today, many younger speakers pronounce *tr* and *dr* words with clusters of /tʃ/ and /dʒ/ plus /r/. See *strong, transport, transit, true* and Chap. 16.

drawing

Newer: /ˈdrɔːrɪŋ/ **ˈdrɔːrɪŋ**
Older: /ˈdrɔːɪŋ/

In the RP era, it was considered wrong ('intrusive') to pronounce a linking /r/ without a corresponding *r* in the spelling. (The reality was that RP speakers did so frequently.) Today, SSB speakers pronounce unwritten linking /r/ unhindered by stigma, for example between the word *draw* and a following vowel, as in *draw it* or *drawing*. See Chap. 25. The quality of the THOUGHT-NORTH vowel is now closer than it was in RP; see Chaps. 4 and 7. Many younger speakers have /dʒr/ in place of /dr/, giving **ˈdʒrɔːrɪŋ**; see Chap. 16. Modern SSB speakers sometimes pronounce the ending *-ing* as /ɪn/ in rapid or casual speech, but this is not a recommendation to the learner; see Chap. 21.

during

Newer: /ˈdʒʊərɪŋ/ **ˈdʒɵːrɪŋ** or **ˈdʒɔːrɪŋ**
Older: /ˈdjʊərɪŋ/

In RP, the preferred pronunciation of this word had a consonant cluster /dj/ followed by the centring diphthong /ʊə/. Today, the affricate /dʒ/ is preferred; see also *education, graduate, institute, situation, tube, Tuesday,* and Chap. 15. The stressed vowel is now a monophthong, some speakers using a central quality and others the THOUGHT-NORTH vowel; see also *poor, sure, tourist, your,* and Chap. 13. Modern SSB speakers sometimes pronounce the ending *-ing* as /ɪn/ in rapid or casual speech, but this is not a recommendation to the learner; see Chap. 21.

education

Newer: e/dʒə/cation **ˌɛdʒəˈkɛjʃən**
Older: e/djʊ/cation

In RP, the preferred pronunciation of this word had a consonant cluster /dj/ followed by the weak FOOT vowel /ʊ/. Today, SSB speakers prefer to use the affricate /dʒ/; see also *during, graduate, institute, situation, tube, Tuesday,* and Chap. 15. In addition, there's a tendency to replace weak /ʊ/ with schwa /ə/ when a consonant follows; see also *particular* and Chap. 10. Both these changes bring the word into line with its American pronunciation; see Chap. 2.

ego

Newer: /ˈiː/go ˈɪjgəw
Older: /ˈe/go

During the RP era, the preferred pronunciation of this word had the DRESS vowel, though a pronunciation with the FLEECE vowel was also common. The word has become more popular in recent decades (referring not to a term in Freudian psychoanalysis but to one's sense of self-esteem), with the FLEECE pronunciation firmly displacing the DRESS form. See also *omega*.

excursion

Newer: excur/ʒən/ əkˈskəːʒən
Older: excur/ʃən/

In RP, the preferred pronunciation of this word contained the voiceless fricative /ʃ/, though a pronunciation with the voiced fricative /ʒ/ was also heard. Today, /ʒ/ is well established, although /ʃ/ is still heard. This change brings the word into line with the American pronunciation. See also *Asia, aversion, version*. The initial vowel may be weak /ə/ or /ɪ/ (see Chap. 10); or the DRESS vowel, as in RP.

exit

Newer: e/gz/it ˈegzɪt
Older: e/ks/it

In RP, the preferred pronunciation of this word contained the voiceless consonant sequence /ks/. In recent decades, a pronunciation with voiced /gz/ has also become popular, though it has not replaced /ks/. The newer form is the preferred pronunciation in America. A similar development has occurred more recently with the coinage *Brexit*: at first, a pronunciation with /ks/ was preferred, but an alternative with /gz/ has rapidly risen in popularity. See *crescent, mausoleum, newspaper, transit*, and Chap. 2.

exquisite

Newer: /əkˈskwɪzɪt/ əkˈskwɪzɪt
Older: /ˈekskwɪzɪt/

In RP, the preferred pronunciation of this word was stressed on the first syllable, though a pronunciation with stress on the second syllable was also heard. Today, the latter pronunciation clearly predominates. See also *applicable, comparable, communal, demonstrable, disciplinary, formidable, omega, quadruple, subsidence* and Chap. 23. The initial vowel may be weak /ə/ or /ɪ/ (see Chap. 10); or the DRESS vowel, as in RP.

false

Newer: /fɒls/ **fɔls**
Older: /fɔːls/

In RP, the preferred pronunciation of this word had the long THOUGHT vowel. More recently there's been a tendency to replace this with the short LOT vowel in common words before /l/ and a following consonant, particularly /t/ or /s/. The THOUGHT pronunciation of *false* is still widely heard. See also *assault, cauldron, halt, salt,* and Chap. 7. (Many speakers vocalize the /l/; see Chap. 20.)

February

Newer: Feb/riː/, Feb/jə/ry, Feb/juːeri:/ **ˈfɛbrɪj, ˈfɛbjərɪj, ˈfɛbjuwɛrɪj**
Older: Feb/ruəri/

Many words have moved closer to the spelling since RP, but *February* has tended to move away from it. Many speakers reduce it to two syllables (or use a syllabic /r/). A substantial number of speakers replace the first /r/ with /j/. Some strengthen the ending *-ary*. The use of /j/ and the strong ending are also preferred by American speakers. See *library, necessary, ordinary, secretary* and Chaps. 2 and 23.

finance (noun and verb)

Newer: /ˈfaɪnæn(t)s/ **ˈfɑjnan(t)s**
Older: /fɪˈnæns/

In older RP, the preferred pronunciation of this word had a weak KIT vowel /ɪ/ in the first syllable. During the twentieth century, an alternative rose in popularity which had a stressed first syllable containing the PRICE diphthong, especially in the noun; this matched the American preference. More recently in SSB, the initial-stressed form has become clearly predominant in both noun and verb, although in America the final-stressed verb is still widely used. Note that the second syllable retains its strong

TRAP vowel, and is not weakened to schwa /ə/. See *cigarette, co-worker, cream cheese, ice cream, princess, protest, research, transport*, and Chaps. 2 and 24. Many SSB speakers now pronounce a /t/ between /n/ and /s/; see *financial, prince, princess, subsidence, transport, violence* and Chap. 17.

financial
Newer: f/aɪ/ˈnancial **fɑjˈnan(t)ʃəl**
Older: f/ɪ/ˈnancial

In older RP, the preferred pronunciation of this word had a weak KIT vowel /ɪ/ in the first syllable. During the twentieth century, this was gradually overtaken by a pronunciation with the PRICE diphthong. The stress pattern remained unchanged. Many SSB speakers now use /ntʃ/ rather than /nʃ/; see *finance, prince, princess, subsidence, transport, violence* and Chap. 17.

forbade
Newer: /fəˈbeɪd/ **fəˈbɛjd**
Older: /fəˈbæd/

In RP, the preferred pronunciation of this word (the past tense of *forbid*) had the TRAP vowel in the second syllable, although an alternative with the FACE vowel also existed. Today the preference is for the latter, which shifts the pronunciation towards the spelling, matching words like *made* and *trade*. See also *ate, bedroom, -day, forehead, handkerchief, hurricane, mayor, mosquito, mushroom, nephew, newspaper, often, portrait*, and Chap. 1.

forehead
Newer: /ˈfɔːhed/ **ˈfoːhɛd**
Older: /ˈfɒrɪd/ or /ˈfɒred/

In RP, the preferred pronunciation of this word had the short LOT vowel in the first syllable, and the secondly syllable could be weak. More recently, speakers have shifted the pronunciation back towards the spelling, so that it matches the pronunciations of the words *before* and *head*. See also *ate, bedroom, -day, forbade, handkerchief, hurricane, mayor, mosquito, mushroom, nephew, newspaper, often, portrait*, and Chap. 1.

foreign

Newer: for/ə/n   **ˈfɔrən**
Older: for/ɪ/n

In RP, the preferred pronunciation of this word contained the weak KIT vowel in the second syllable. Today, the preferred pronunciation has schwa. See *arbitrary, graduate, hatred, interest, interpret, magnet, memento, necklace, secret, separate, system, wireless,* and Chap. 10.

formidable

Newer: forˈmidable   **fəˈmɪdəbəl**
Older: ˈformidable

In RP, the preferred pronunciation of this word had initial stress followed by three weak syllables. Today the preferred pronunciation has stress on the second syllable. See also *applicable, comparable, communal, demonstrable, disciplinary, exquisite, omega, quadruple, subsidence,* and Chaps. 2 and 23.

garage

Newer: /ˈgærɪdʒ/   **ˈgarɪdʒ**
Older: /ˈgærɑːʒ/

In the RP pronunciation, this loanword had an ending similar to the French original, with an open vowel and the final fricative /ʒ/. Today, the preferred pronunciation is nativized, so that the ending is pronounced as in *image, manage* and *village*. (The fricative /ʒ/ does not occur finally in native English words.)

a good deal

Newer: a goo/d d/eal   **əˌgødˈdɪjl**
Older: a goo/d/eal

In RP, the quantifier *a good deal* was often pronounced with a single /d/ when modifying a comparative, e.g. *a good deal more, a good deal better*. Today this is old-fashioned, and a pronunciation with both /d/ phonemes (phonetically a geminate) is now usual. This brings the pronunciation into line with the written form; see Chap. 1.

got, gotten

Newer: gotten ˈgɔtən

Older: got

In RP, the past participle of *get* was *got*, e.g. *it's got colder*. The old form *gotten* fell out of use in Britain long ago, but survived in America. Today, *got* is still the most widely used form in Britain, but *gotten* is heard quite often from younger speakers, probably a result of American influence. See, among many other words, *cigarette, co-worker, debris, (Br)exit, harass, necessary, research*; and Chap. 2.

graduate (noun, adjective)

Newer: gra/dʒuːət/ ˈgradʒʉwət

Older: gra/djʊɪt/

In RP, this word had the approximant /j/, and weak /ʊ/ and /ɪ/ in succession. Today, the preferred pronunciation has (1) the affricate /dʒ/ (see Chap. 15), (2) the weak GOOSE vowel (the FOOT vowel now requires a following consonant; see Chap. 9), and (3) schwa in the final syllable (see Chap. 10). In verbs, the suffix *-ate* has a strong final syllable containing the FACE vowel.

graph

Newer: /grɑːf/ or /græf/ **grɑːf** or **graf**

Older: /græf/

In RP, this word was pronounced with the short TRAP vowel. Today, speakers in the south of England prefer the long PALM vowel, bringing the word into line with *calf, giraffe, half, laugh* and *staff*. Nonetheless, the TRAP pronunciation of *graph* survives in America and the north of England; both pronunciations can now be considered standard. See *bath*, and Chap. 11.

halt

Newer: h/ɒ/lt **hɔlt**

Older: h/ɔː/lt

In RP, the preferred pronunciation of this word had the long THOUGHT vowel. Today, many speakers replace this with the short LOT vowel in common words before /l/ and a following consonant, particularly /t/ or /s/.

In *halt*, LOT is now preferred. See also *assault, cauldron, false, salt,* and Chap. 7. (Many speakers vocalize the /l/; see Chap. 20.)

handkerchief
Newer: handkerch/iː/f **'haŋkətʃɹjf**
Older: handkerch/ɪ/f

In RP, this word was pronounced with the weak KIT vowel /ɪ/ in the final syllable. Today, the FLEECE vowel is more common, bringing the pronunciation closer to the spelling, so that the final syllable now matches the word *chief*. The preferred pronunciation in America retains the KIT vowel. (Some British speakers also shift *mischief* from KIT to FLEECE, but this isn't so common.) See also *ate, bedroom, -day, forbade, forehead, hurricane, mayor, mosquito, mushroom, nephew, newspaper, often, portrait,* and Chap. 1.

happy
Newer: happ/iː/ **'hapɪj**
Older: happ/ɪ/

For most of the RP era, this word and thousands of others, mostly written with *-y* but also including *coffee, money, prairie, taxi,* etc., were pronounced with a final KIT vowel /ɪ/. This has been firmly replaced in modern SSB with the FLEECE diphthong. See for example *arbitrarily, arbitrary, controversy, disciplinary, February, Italy, necessarily, necessary, ordinary, primarily, secretary, temporarily, temporary, voluntarily,* and Chaps. 5 and 8.

harass
Newer: /həˈræs/ **həˈras**
Older: /ˈhærəs/

In RP, this word was stressed on the first syllable, with schwa in the second. In contemporary pronunciation this is reversed, with stress on the second syllable and schwa in the first, as in America; see Chap. 2. Note that the major pronouncing dictionaries stick to /ˈhærəs/ as their first recommendation, warning moreover that the modern pronunciation 'evokes negative feelings among those who use the traditional form'

(Longman) and is 'strongly disliked by more conservative speakers' (Cambridge). The modern learner may disregard such dated attitudes.

hatred
Newer: hatr/ə/d 'hɛjtrəd
Older: hatr/ɪ/d

In RP, the preferred pronunciation of this word contained the weak KIT vowel in the ending. It's now increasingly pronounced with schwa, though KIT is still used by many speakers. See also *arbitrary, foreign, graduate, interest, interpret, magnet, memento, necklace, secret, separate, system, wireless* and Chap. 10. Many younger speakers have /tʃr/ in place of /tr/, giving 'hɛjtʃrəd; see Chap. 16.

here
Newer: **hɪː** or hɪjə
Older: /hɪə/

In RP, *here* and other words in the NEAR set contained a centring diphthong, /ɪə/. Today, NEAR words are often heard with a tense vowel followed by schwa (which may be disyllabic) or with a smoothed long monophthong. The most frequently-occurring NEAR words, such as *here*, are very widely pronounced with the long monophthong. See also *idea, year*, and Chaps. 12 and 13. (An earlier RP variant, /hjəː/, faded away during the twentieth century.)

hurricane
Newer: hurric/eɪ/n 'hʌrɪkɛjn
Older: hurric/ə/n

In RP, the preferred pronunciation of this word had schwa /ə/ in the final syllable. Today, the strong FACE vowel is more common, bringing the pronunciation closer to the spelling, so that the final syllable now matches the word *cane*; this also matches the American pronunciation. See also *ate, bedroom, -day, forbade, forehead, handkerchief, mayor, mosquito, mushroom, nephew, newspaper, often, portrait*, and Chap. 1.

ice cream
Newer: 'ice ˌcream 'ajs ˌkrɪjm
Older: ˌice 'cream

In RP, the main stress on this compound noun belonged to the word *cream*. The majority pronunciation in Britain today, except among older people, has the main stress on *ice*, as in America. See also *cigarette, co-worker, cream cheese, finance, princess, protest, research, transport*, and Chaps. 2 and 24.

idea

Newer: **ɑjˈdɪː** or **ɑjˈdɪjə**
Older: /aɪˈdɪə/

In RP, *idea* and other words in the NEAR set contained a centring diphthong, /ɪə/. Today, NEAR words are often heard with a tense vowel followed by schwa (which may be disyllabic) or with a smoothed long monophthong. The most frequently-occurring NEAR words, such as *idea*, are very widely pronounced with the long monophthong. See also *here, year*, and Chaps. 12 and 13.

important

Newer: import[ən]t **ɪmˈpoːtənt**
Older: import[n̩]t

In RP, this word was typically pronounced with a nasally released [t] followed by a syllabic nasal. In contemporary speech, the pronunciation with a normally released [t] followed by a schwa is increasingly heard, and is perhaps already more common. See *Italy, ordinary* and Chap. 18.

institute

Newer: insti/tʃ/ute **ˈɪnstɪtʃʉwt**
Older: insti/tj/ute

In RP, the preferred pronunciation of this word contained a two-consonant cluster /tj/. In contemporary speech, this cluster is increasingly replaced by the single affricate /tʃ/. This is especially true in unstressed syllables. See *during, education, graduate, situation, tube, Tuesday*, and Chap. 15.

interpret

Newer: interpr/ə/t **ɪnˈtəːprət**
Older: interpr/ɪ/t

In RP, the preferred pronunciation of this word contained the weak KIT vowel in the ending. Today, the preferred pronunciation has schwa;

see *arbitrary, foreign, graduate, hatred, interest, magnet, memento, necklace, secret, separate, system, wireless,* and Chap. 10.

interest
Newer: int/rest/ 'ɪntrɛst or 'ɪntrəst
Older: int/rɪst/

The final syllable of this word has long been variable, featuring the KIT vowel, the DRESS vowel, or schwa. However, the KIT vowel, which was preferred in RP, has increasingly been displaced by the strong DRESS vowel. A form with a weak second syllable is still heard, but is more likely to contain schwa; see Chap. 10. Many younger speakers have /tʃr/ in place of /tr/, giving 'ɪntʃrest; see Chap. 16.

Italy
Newer: It[əl]y 'ɪtəlɪj
Older: It[l]y

In RP, this word was often pronounced with a laterally released [t] followed by a syllabic lateral. In contemporary speech, a pronunciation with a normally released [t] followed by a schwa is preferred. See *important* and Chap. 18.

library
Newer: /'laɪbriː/ 'lɑjbrɪj
Older: /'laɪbrərɪ/

In RP, the preferred pronunciation of this word ended in two weak syllables. Today it's mostly heard as a two-syllable word, avoiding two successive /r/ consonants. See also *arbitrary* and Chap. 23.

magnet
Newer: magn/ə/t 'magnət
Older: magn/ɪ/t

In RP, the preferred pronunciation of this word contained the weak KIT vowel in the ending. Today, the preferred pronunciation has schwa; see *arbitrary, foreign, graduate, hatred, interest, interpret, memento, necklace, secret, separate, system, wireless,* and Chap. 10.

mausoleum

Newer: mau/zəˈliːəm/ ˌ**moːzəˈlɪjəm**
Older: mau/səˈlɪəm/

In RP, the preferred pronunciation of this word contained the voiceless fricative /s/. Today, the preferred pronunciation has the voiced fricative /z/; see *crescent, exit, newspaper, transit*, and Chap. 2. The RP-era transcription /ɪə/ was ambiguous, since it could stand for a single centring diphthong or for a two-syllable sequence of /ɪ/ plus /ə/. In the modern pronunciation, the stressed syllable contains the FLEECE diphthong, /ɪ/ being no longer permitted before a vowel; see *delirious, various* and Chap. 8.

mayor

Newer: /ˈmeɪə/ ˈ**mɛjə**
Older: /meə/

In RP, this word was pronounced as one syllable with the SQUARE diphthong. Many speakers retain a one-syllable pronunciation with the modern SQUARE vowel, **mɛː**, but younger speakers increasingly pronounce *mayor* as two syllables, with the FACE vowel followed by schwa. This change brings the pronunciation closer to the spelling and to the American pronunciation. See also *ate, bedroom, forbade, forehead, handkerchief, hurricane, mosquito, mushroom, nephew, newspaper, often, portrait*, and Chaps. 1 and 2.

memento

Newer: m/ə/mento **məˈmɛntəw**
Older: m/ɪ/mento

In RP, the preferred pronunciation of this word contained the weak KIT vowel in the first syllable. Today, the preferred pronunciation has schwa. See *arbitrary, foreign, graduate, hatred, interest, interpret, magnet, necklace, secret, separate, system, wireless*, and Chap. 10.

mosquito

Newer: m/ɒ/squito **məˈskɪjtəw**
Older: m/ə/squito

In RP, this word was pronounced with schwa /ə/ in the first syllable. Today, the strong LOT vowel is more common, bringing the pronunciation closer to the spelling, so that the beginning now matches the words *moss* and *mosque.* (Americans, on the other hand, prefer schwa.) See also *ate, bedroom, forbade, -day, forehead, handkerchief, hurricane, mayor, mushroom, nephew, often, newspaper, portrait,* and Chaps. 1 and 2.

mushroom
Newer: mushr/uː/m ˈmʌʃrʉwm
Older: mushr/ʊ/m

In RP, the preferred pronunciation of this word had the short FOOT vowel /ʊ/ in the second syllable. Today the preferred pronunciation has the long GOOSE vowel. This brings the word into line with the preferred pronunciation of *room,* and with the most common pronunciation of the spelling 'oo'. See *ate, bedroom, -day, forbade, forehead, handkerchief, hurricane, mayor, mosquito, nephew, newspaper, often, portrait* and Chap. 1.

necessarily
Newer: ˌne/sə'se/rily ˌnɛsəˈsɛrəlɪj
Older: ˈne/sɪs(ə)/rily

In RP, the preferred pronunciation of this word had initial stress followed by three or even four weak syllables: /ˈnesɪs(ə)rɪlɪ/. Today, the preferred pronunciation has primary stress on the antepenultimate syllable, which contains the DRESS vowel, like the American pronunciation. See also *arbitrarily, primarily, temporarily, voluntarily,* and Chaps. 2 and 23.

necessary
Newer: ˈne/səse/ry ˈnɛsəsɛrɪj
Older: ˈne/sɪs(ə)/ry

In RP, the preferred pronunciation of this word had initial stress followed by two or three weak syllables: /ˈnesɪs(ə)rɪ/. Today, the preferred pronunciation has a strong third syllable, containing the DRESS vowel, like the American pronunciation. See also *February, ordinary, secretary,* and Chaps. 2 and 23.

necklace
Newer: neckl/ə/s ˈnɛkləs
Older: neckl/ɪ/s

In RP, the preferred pronunciation of this word contained the weak KIT vowel in the second syllable. Today, the preferred pronunciation has schwa; see *arbitrary, foreign, graduate, hatred, interest, interpret, magnet, memento, secret, separate, system, wireless,* and Chap. 10.

nephew

Newer: ne/f/ew ˈ**nɛfjʉw**
Older: ne/v/ew

In RP, the preferred pronunciation of this word had a voiced fricative. Today, the word is pronounced with a voiceless fricative, bringing the pronunciation closer to the spelling, as 'ph' generally corresponds to /f/. This also matches the American pronunciation. See also *ate, bedroom, -day, forbade, forehead, handkerchief, hurricane, mayor, mosquito, mushroom, often, newspaper, portrait,* and Chaps. 1 and 2.

newspaper

Newer: new/z/paper ˈ**njʉwzpɛjpə**
Older: new/s/paper

In RP, the preferred pronunciation of this word had the voiceless fricative /s/. Today, the preferred pronunciation has the voiced fricative /z/; see also *crescent, exit, mausoleum, transit.* This change brings the pronunciation into line with the word *news,* and with the preferred American pronunciation; see *ate, bedroom, -day, forbade, forehead, handkerchief, hurricane, mayor, mosquito, mushroom, nephew, often, portrait,* and Chaps. 1 and 2.

often

Newer: of/tən/ ˈ**ɔftən**
Older: of/ən/

RP speakers preferred to pronounce this word without any /t/. Today, it's widely heard with a pronounced /t/, bringing the pronunciation into line with the spelling. This is most common with younger speakers; the pronunciation without /t/ is still widely heard. See also *ate, bedroom, -day, forbade, forehead, handkerchief, hurricane, mayor, mosquito, mushroom, nephew, newspaper, portrait,* and Chap. 1.

old

Newer: /ɒld/ **ɔld**
Older: /əʊld/

In RP, this word was pronounced with the GOAT diphthong, beginning with a schwa-type quality, [əʊ]. In contemporary pronunciation, such a diphthong is considered old-fashioned before syllable-final dark /l/. In this environment, many younger speakers instead use the short LOT vowel. It's also common to hear an intermediate diphthong, [ɔʊ] or [ɔw], before the dark /l/. See also *whole*, and Chaps. 6 and 7. (Many speakers vocalize the /l/, [ɔwd]; see Chap. 20.)

omega

Newer: oˈmega **ə(w)ˈmɪjgə** or **ə(w)ˈmɛjgə**
Older: ˈomega

In RP, the preferred pronunciation of this word had initial stress. This is still heard, but today there's a widespread alternative with stress on the second syllable. See also *applicable, comparable, communal, demonstrable, disciplinary, exquisite, formidable, quadruple, subsidence,* and Chap. 23. The stressed vowel is usually FLEECE (see also *ego*), but the FACE vowel is also heard.

one

Newer: /wɒn/ **wɔn**
Older: /wʌn/

In RP, this word was pronounced with the STRUT vowel /ʌ/, so that it rhymed with *done*. This pronunciation is still widespread, but a common alternative has the LOT vowel, making the word rhyme with *gone*.

ordinary

Newer: or/dɪn/ry or ordin/e/ry ˈɔːdɪnrɪj or ˈɔːdɪnɛrɪj
Older: or/dn̩/ry

In RP, the preferred pronunciation of this word contained a syllabic nasal followed by /r/. This pronunciation is still very common, but the word is also widely heard with a normally-released /d/ followed by a weak KIT vowel, and/or a strong ending containing the DRESS vowel. These two vowel restorations bring the pronunciation more into line with the spelling; the second brings it into line with the American pronunciation.

See also *important*, *Italy*, and Chap. 18; and *February*, *necessary*, *secretary*, and Chaps. 2 and 23.

other
Newer: o/v/er ˈʌvə
Older: o/ð/er

The newer pronunciation is by no means a new standard: the version with /ð/ remains more common and more prestigious. However, words pronounced with TH-fronting are increasingly heard from speakers whose accent is otherwise SSB, including documentary and news presenters, *other* being perhaps the most common. See Chap. 22.

our
Newer: ɑː
Older: /aʊə/

In RP, this word was pronounced with two syllables, identical to *hour*, and rhyming with *flower*; RP speakers could also smooth it to [aə]. Today, a pronunciation like *hour* can still be heard, but very commonly the word is pronounced simply as the PALM-START vowel. Note that the modern two-syllable version is **awə**; frequently this is transformed by contemporary smoothing into [aː]; as a result, monophthongal pronunciations of this word clearly predominate. See Chap. 12.

paragon
Newer: parag/ɒn/ ˈparəgɒn
Older: parag/ən/

In RP, this word was pronounced with a weak final syllable containing schwa /ə/. Today it's also widely heard with the strong LOT vowel. This change brings the word into line with the American pronunciation. See also *aeon, pentagon, polygon* and Chap. 2.

particular
Newer: partic/jə/lar pəˈtɪkjələ
Older: partic/jʊ/lar

In RP, this word was pronounced with the weak FOOT vowel /ʊ/ in the third syllable. Today, this vowel is increasingly replaced with schwa /ə/ when a consonant follows; see also *education* and Chap. 10.

patriot

Newer: p/eɪ/triot **ˈpɛjtrɪjət**
Older: p/æ/triot

In RP, the preferred pronunciations of this word had the TRAP vowel in the first syllable, as in *Patrick*. Today, in the noun *patriot*, speakers strongly prefer the FACE vowel, as in *hatred*, *matrix* and *patron*. In the adjective *patriotic*, the TRAP pronunciation is still heard, but the FACE pronunciation is becoming more common. This change brings British pronunciation into line with the American pronunciation; see Chap. 2. Many younger speakers have /tʃr/ in place of /tr/, giving **ˈpɛjtʃrɪjət**; see Chap. 16.

pentagon

Newer: pentag/ɒn/ **ˈpɛntəgɔn**
Older: pentag/ən/

In RP, this word was pronounced with a weak final syllable containing schwa /ə/. Today it's also widely heard with the strong LOT vowel. This change brings the word into line with the American pronunciation. See also *aeon, paragon, polygon* and Chap. 2.

polygon

Newer: polyg/ɒn/ **ˈpɔlɪjgɔn**
Older: polyg/ən/

In RP, this word was pronounced with a weak final syllable containing schwa /ə/. Today it's also widely heard with the strong LOT vowel. This change brings the word into line with the American pronunciation. See also *aeon, paragon, pentagon* and Chap. 2. (The second vowel is heard as both FLEECE and KIT.)

pool

Newer: /pɔːl/ **poːl**
Older: /puːl/

In RP, the preferred pronunciation of this word had the back GOOSE vowel, /uː/. The GOOSE vowel is now generally central, except that it's backed before a dark /l/, as in *pool*. For a number of younger speakers this back vowel is merged with the modern THOUGHT vowel [o:], merging *pool* with *Paul*. See also *cool, school, you'll* and Chap. 6.

poor

Newer: /pɔː/ **pɔː**
Older: /pʊə/

In RP, the preferred pronunciation of this word had the centring diphthong /ʊə/. In contemporary SSB, the preferred pronunciation has the THOUGHT-NORTH monophthong, making this word identical in pronunciation to *pour, pore* and *paw*. See also *during, sure, tourist, your,* and Chap. 13. The quality of the modern THOUGHT-NORTH vowel is closer than in RP; see Chaps. 4 and 7.

portrait

Newer: portr/eɪ/t **ˈpɔːtrɛjt**
Older: portr/ɪ/t or portr/ə/t

In RP, this word was pronounced with weak /ɪ/ or /ə/ in the final syllable. Today, the strong FACE vowel is more common, bringing the pronunciation closer to the spelling, so that the final syllable now matches the word *trait*. (In America the weak second syllable is still preferred.) See also *ate, bedroom, -day, forbade, forehead, handkerchief, hurricane, mayor, mosquito, mushroom, nephew, newspaper, often,* and Chap. 1. Many younger speakers have /tʃr/ in place of /tr/, giving **ˈpɔːtʃrɛjt**; see Chap. 16.

potpourri

Newer: ˌpotpouˈrri **ˌpəwpəˈrɪj**
Older: ˌpotˈpourri

In RP, the preferred pronunciation of this loanword from French had the main stress on the second syllable, /ˌpəʊˈpʊ(ə)rɪ/ or /ˌpəʊˈpʊ(ə)riː/. Today the word is stressed on the final syllable, matching the most common stress pattern in America. See *debris* and Chap. 2.

primarily

Newer: /praɪˈme/rily **prajˈmɛrəlɪj**
Older: /ˈpraɪmə/rily

In RP, the preferred pronunciation of this word had initial stress followed by three weak syllables. Today, this has been almost completely replaced by a pronunciation with stress on the second syllable which contains the DRESS vowel, as in America. See also *arbitrarily, necessarily, temporarily, voluntarily,* and Chaps. 2 and 23.

prince

Newer: prin/ts/ **prɪnts**
Older: prin/s/

In RP, this word was pronounced with /n/ followed directly by /s/. This pronunciation is still common, but many speakers now pronounce an 'epenthetic' /t/ between /n/ and /s/, making the word identical to *prints*; see *finance, financial, princess, subsidence, transport, violence* and Chap. 17.

princess

Newer: /ˈprɪn(t)ses/ **ˈprɪn(t)sɛs**
Older: /prɪnˈses/

In RP, the preferred pronunciation of this word had primary stress on the final syllable. Today, a pronunciation with stress on the first syllable is more common, as in America. See *cigarette, co-worker, cream cheese, finance, ice cream, protest, research, transport,* and Chaps. 2 and 24. Many speakers now pronounce a /t/ between /n/ and /s/ before an unstressed vowel; see *finance, financial, prince, subsidence, transport, violence* and Chap. 17.

protest (verb)

Newer: /ˈprəʊ/test **ˈprəʊtɛst**
Older: /prəˈtest

In RP, the preferred pronunciation of this word had final stress and a weak schwa /ə/ in the first syllable. Today, it's also commonly pronounced like the noun *protest*, with a stressed first syllable containing the GOAT diphthong; the second syllable retains its strong DRESS vowel, and isn't weakened to /ə/ or /ɪ/. See *cigarette, co-worker, cream cheese, finance, ice cream, princess, research, transport,* and Chaps. 2 and 24. The quality of the DRESS vowel is now opener than it was in RP; see Chap. 4.

quadruple

Newer: /kwɒˈdruːpəl/ **kwɔˈdrʉwpəl**
Older: /ˈkwɒdrʊpəl/

In RP, the preferred pronunciation of this word had stress on the first syllable, which was followed by two weak syllables. Today, the word is generally pronounced with stress on the middle syllable, which contains the GOOSE vowel. See also *applicable, comparable, communal, demonstrable, disciplinary, exquisite, formidable, omega, subsidence,* and Chap. 23.

real

Newer: /riː(ə)l/ **ˈrɪj(ə)l**
Older: /rɪəl/

In RP, the preferred pronunciation of *real* was different from that of *reel*: they were /rɪəl/ and /riːl/ respectively. Today, these two words are generally pronounced the same, with the FLEECE vowel. A schwa is often heard before the final /l/, as a result of 'pre-l breaking'.

research (noun & verb)

Newer: /ˈriːsɜːtʃ/ **ˈrɪjsəːtʃ**
Older: /rɪˈsɜːtʃ/

In RP, the preferred pronunciation of this word had final stress and a weak KIT vowel /ɪ/ in the first syllable, especially in the case of the verb. Today, both noun and verb are also widely heard with a stressed first syllable containing the FLEECE vowel. This brings the pronunciation into line with American English. (Final stress is somewhat more likely in the verb than the noun, and in the speech of academics.) See *cigarette, co-worker, cream cheese, ice cream, princess, protest, transport,* and Chaps. 2 and 24.

salt

Newer: /sɒlt/ **sɔlt**
Older: /sɔːlt/

In RP, the preferred pronunciation of this word had the long THOUGHT vowel. Today, many speakers replace this with the short LOT vowel in common words before /l/ and a following consonant, particularly /t/ or /s/.

In *salt*, LOT is now preferred. See also *assault, cauldron, false, halt,* and Chap. 7. (Many speakers vocalize the /l/; see Chap. 20.)

school

Newer: /skɔːl/ **skoːl**
Older: /skuːl/

In RP, the preferred pronunciation of this word had the back GOOSE vowel, /uː/. The GOOSE vowel is now generally central, except that it's backed before a dark /l/, as in *school*. For a number of younger speakers, this back vowel is merged with the modern THOUGHT vowel [oː]. See also *cool, pool, you'll* and Chap. 6.

secret

Newer: secr/ə/t **ˈsɪjkrət**
Older: secr/ɪ/t

In RP, the preferred pronunciation of this word contained the weak KIT vowel in the ending. Today, the preferred pronunciation has schwa; see *arbitrary, foreign, graduate, hatred, interest, interpret, magnet, memento, necklace, separate, system, wireless,* and Chap. 10.

secretary

Newer: secre/ter/y **ˈsɛkrətɛrɪj**
Older: secre/tr/y

In RP, this word was generally pronounced as three syllables, /ˈsekrətrɪ/. This pronunciation is still common, but a four-syllable pronunciation is also widely heard, especially among younger speakers, with a strong DRESS vowel in the ending *-ary*, as in American English. See also *February, necessary, ordinary,* and Chaps. 2 and 23.

separate (adjective)

Newer: sep/rət/ **ˈsɛprət**
Older: sep/rɪt/

In RP, the preferred pronunciation of this word had the weak KIT vowel in the ending *-ate*. Today, schwa is preferred. See *arbitrary, foreign, graduate, hatred, interest, interpret, magnet, memento, necklace, secret, system, wireless,* and Chap. 10. In verbs, the suffix *-ate* has a strong final syllable containing the FACE vowel.

situation
Newer: si/tʃ/uation ˌsɪtʃʉwˈɛjʃən
Older: si/tj/uation
In RP, the preferred pronunciation of this word contained a two-consonant cluster /tj/. In contemporary SSB, this cluster is increasingly replaced by the single affricate /tʃ/, especially in unstressed syllables. See *during, education, institute, situation, tube, Tuesday,* and Chap. 15. In RP, the second vowel was the FOOT vowel /ʊ/, but today the FOOT vowel requires a following consonant, and the modern pronunciation has the weak GOOSE vowel; see *graduate* and Chap. 9.

sonorous
Newer: /ˈsɒnərəs/ ˈsɔnərəs
Older: /səˈnɔːrəs/
The preferred RP pronunciation of this word for most of the twentieth century had stress on the second syllable, so that the word rhymed with *porous* and *chorus*. In recent decades, an alternative with initial stress has firmly replaced it as the preferred pronunciation. This is despite a tendency for stress to move in the opposite direction, as in *communal*; see Chap. 23.

strong
Newer: /ʃ/trong ʃtʃrɔŋ
Older: /s/trong
In RP, the cluster /tr/ was pronounced as a postalveolar affricate, but at a phonemic level began with /t/. Today, many younger speakers pronounce *tr* as a cluster of /tʃ/ and /r/; these speakers may pronounce *str* clusters with /ʃ/ rather than /s/. See *drive, transit, true* and Chap. 16.

subsidence
Newer: /səbˈsaɪ/dence səbˈsɑjdən(t)s
Older: /ˈsʌbsɪ/dence
In RP, the preferred pronunciation of this word was stressed on the first syllable, though a pronunciation with stress on the second syllable was also heard. Today, the preference is for the latter. See also *applicable, comparable, communal, demonstrable, disciplinary, exquisite, formidable, omega, quadruple,* and Chap. 23. Many SSB speakers now pronounce a

/t/ between /n/ and /s/; see *finance, financial, prince, princess, transport, violence* and Chap. 17.

suit, suitable, suitcase; super, supermarket, supervise

Newer: /suː/ **sʉw**

Older: /sjuː/

The traditional RP pronunciation of these words began with the consonant sequence /sj/. During the later RP period, this was decisively superseded by a pronunciation without /j/. Today, word-initial /sj/ is generally perceived as very old-fashioned. See Chap. 15.

sure

Newer: /ʃɔː/ **ʃoː**

Older: /ʃʊə/

In RP, the preferred pronunciation of this word contained the centring diphthong /ʊə/. However, an alternative pronunciation with the THOUGHT-NORTH monophthong was already common among speakers of RP, and today the latter is far more common. See also *during, poor, tourist, your*, and Chap. 13. The quality of the modern THOUGHT-NORTH vowel is closer than in RP; see Chaps. 4 and 7.

system

Newer: syst/ə/m **ˈsɪstəm**

Older: syst/ɪ/m

In RP, the preferred pronunciation of this word contained the weak KIT vowel in the ending. Today, the preferred pronunciation has schwa; see *arbitrary, foreign, graduate, hatred, interest, interpret, magnet, memento, necklace, secret, separate, wireless*, and Chap. 10

temporarily

Newer: /ˌtempəˈrerəliː/ **ˌtɛmpəˈrerəlɪj**

Older: /ˈtempərərɪlɪ/

In RP, the preferred pronunciation of this word had initial stress, which could be followed by four successive weak syllables. Today the clearly preferred pronunciation, as in America, has primary stress on the antepenultimate syllable, which contains the strong DRESS vowel. See also *arbitrarily, necessarily, primarily, voluntarily* and Chap. 23.

temporary
Newer: /ˈtemp(ə)riː/ **ˈtɛmp(ə)rɪj**
Older: /ˈtemprərɪ/

In RP, the preferred pronunciation of this word had two /r/ consonants. Today it's mostly heard without the first /r/, though some use the older pronunciation, especially in careful speech. See also *arbitrary, library, necessary* and Chap. 23.

thank you
Newer: thank/juː/ **ˈθaŋkjʉw**
Older: thank/jʊ/

In RP, *thank you* ended in the lax FOOT vowel /ʊ/. Today, the word ends in the GOOSE vowel; indeed, in modern SSB the FOOT vowel only occurs before a consonant. See *graduate*, and Chap. 9.

the
Newer: before vowels **ðɪj** or **ðə[ʔ]**
Older: before vowels /ðɪ/

In RP, the unstressed definite article *the* was pronounced before consonants with a schwa /ðə/, and before vowels with the weak KIT vowel /ðɪ/. Today, the pre-consonantal pronunciation is still **ðə**. But before vowels we hear either the FLEECE vowel, e.g. *the address* **ðɪjəˈdrɛs**; or, increasingly from younger speakers, the schwa form followed by glottal stop, e.g. *the address* **ðə[ʔ]əˈdrɛs**. The latter form is more established in America. See Chaps. 8 and 26.

tourist
Newer: t/ɔː/rist **ˈtoːrɪst**
Older: t/ʊə/rist

In RP, the preferred pronunciation of this word contained the centring diphthong /ʊə/. Today, an alternative pronunciation with the THOUGHT-NORTH monophthong is very common, especially among younger speakers. See also *during, poor, sure, your*, and Chap. 13. The quality of the modern THOUGHT-NORTH vowel is closer than in RP; see Chaps. 4 and 7.

transit
Newer: tran/z/it **ˈtranzɪt**
Older: tran/s/it

In RP, the preferred pronunciation of this word had the voiceless fricative /s/. Today the preferred pronunciation has the voiced fricative /z/; see also *crescent, exit, mausoleum, newspaper*. Today, many younger speakers pronounce *tr* words with /tʃ/ plus /r/, giving ˈtʃranzɪt. See *drive, strong, transport, true,* and Chap. 16.

transport (verb)

Newer: ˈtransport ˈtran(t)spoːt
Older: tranˈsport

In RP, this verb was pronounced with final stress. Today, it's also commonly pronounced with initial stress, like the noun *transport*; the same is true in America. However, stress on the second syllable continues to be more common in the suffixed form *tranˈsported*. See *cigarette, co-worker, cream cheese, finance, ice cream, princess, protest, research,* and Chaps. 2 and 24. Today, many younger speakers pronounce *tr* words with /tʃ/ plus /r/, giving ˈtʃran(t)spoːt; see *drive, strong, transit, true,* and Chap. 16. Many SSB speakers now pronounce a /t/ between /n/ and /s/; see *finance, financial, prince, princess, subsidence, transport, violence* and Chap. 17.

true

Newer: /tʃ/rue tʃrʉw
Older: /t/rue

In RP, /tr/ and /dr/ clusters were pronounced as postalveolar affricates, but at a phonemic level began with /t/ and /d/. Today, many younger speakers pronounce *tr* and *dr* words with clusters of /tʃ/ and /dʒ/ plus /r/. See *drive, strong, transit, transport* and Chap. 16.

tube

Newer: /tʃ/ube tʃʉwb
Older: /tj/ube

In RP, the preferred pronunciation of the word *tube* had a consonant cluster /tj/. Today, /tj/ is still widely heard, but the preference in *tube* (and *YouTube*), particularly among younger speakers, is for the affricate /tʃ/. See also *during, education, graduate, institute, situation, Tuesday,* and Chap. 15. (The preferred American pronunciation of *tube* begins simply with /t/, so that the word begins like *two*.)

Tuesday

Newer: /tʃ/uesday ˈt**ʃʉwzdɛj**
Older: /tj/uesday

In RP, the preferred pronunciation of this word had a consonant cluster /tj/. Today, the preference is for the affricate /tʃ/, though /tj/ is still widely heard; see also *during, graduate, education, institute, situation, tube,* and Chap. 15. (The preferred American pronunciation begins simply /t/, so that the word begins like *two*.) The final syllable was usually /dɪ/ in RP, but now the FACE vowel is preferred; see *-day* and Chap. 1.

various

Newer: ˈv**ɛːrɪjəs**
Older: /ˈveərɪəs/

In RP, the stressed vowel of this word was a centring diphthong, /eə/. This SQUARE vowel has steadily monophthongized since RP; see Chap. 13. The RP-era transcription /ɪə/ was ambiguous, since it could stand for a single centring diphthong or for a two-syllable sequence of /ɪ/ plus /ə/. Today the ending is disyllabic, with the weak FLEECE diphthong before schwa, /ɪ/ no longer being permitted before a vowel. See *delirious, mausoleum* and Chap. 8.

version

Newer: ver/ʒən/ ˈv**əːʒən**
Older: ver/ʃən/

The RP pronunciation of this word contained the voiceless fricative /ʃ/. In recent decades, an alternative with /ʒ/ has risen in popularity, though the pronunciation with /ʃ/ is still very widely heard. The newer pronunciation is also the one preferred in America. See also *Asia, aversion, excursion,* and Chap. 2.

violence

Newer: /ˈvaɪ/lence ˈv**ɑjlən(t)s**
Older: /ˈvaɪə/lence

In RP, this word was pronounced with three syllables, though it could be smoothed to [vaələns] (see Chap. 12). This is still the majority pronunciation, but increasingly the word may be heard, especially from younger speakers, as two syllables without the middle schwa. This is also true of the adjective *violent*. See also *diamond* and Chap. 23. Many SSB speakers now pronounce a /t/ between /n/ and /s/; see *finance, financial, prince, princess, transport, subsidence* and Chap. 17.

voluntarily

Newer: ˌvolun/ˈte/rily **ˌvɔlənˈtɛrəlɪj**
Older: ˈvolun/t(ə)/rily

In RP, the preferred pronunciation of this word had initial stress followed by three or four weak syllables: /ˈvɒlənt(ə)rɪlɪ/. Today, the preferred pronunciation has main stress on the third syllable, which contains the DRESS vowel, as in America. See also *arbitrarily, necessarily, primarily, temporarily,* and Chaps. 2 and 23.

what, when, which, while, etc.

Newer: /w/
Older: /hw/

The sequence /hw/ faded from widespread use in Southern Britain long ago, during the RP period. It survives in some other accents, notably Scottish English. On the other hand, /hj/ survives robustly in SSB before the GOOSE vowel, and should be pronounced in *human, Hugh, huge, humour,* etc.

whole

Newer: /hɒl/ **hɔl**
Older: /həʊl/

In RP, this word was pronounced with the GOAT diphthong, beginning with a schwa-type quality, [əʊ]. In contemporary pronunciation, such a diphthong is considered old-fashioned before syllable-final dark /l/. In this environment, many younger speakers instead use the short LOT vowel. It's also common to hear an intermediate diphthong, [ɔʊ] or [ɔw], before the dark /l/. See also *old,* and Chaps. 6 and 7. (Many speakers vocalize the /l/, [ɔwd]; see Chap. 20.)

wireless

Newer: wirel/ə/s **ˈwajələs**
Older: wirel/ɪ/s

In RP, the preferred pronunciation of this word contained the weak KIT vowel in the ending. Today, *-less* is also very often heard with schwa. See *arbitrary, foreign, graduate, hatred, interest, interpret, magnet, memento,* *necklace, secret, separate, system,* and Chap. 10. (Note also that in Britain during the RP era, the word *wireless* was generally used to mean 'radio', but that usage is now very old-fashioned.)

year

Newer: **jɪː** or **jɪjə**

Older: /jɜː/ or /jɪə/

In RP, the preferred pronunciation of this word contained the NURSE vowel, which was transcribed as either /jəː/ or /jɜː/ (see Chap. 4). This pronunciation has now markedly fallen out of use. An alternative RP pronunciation contained RP's NEAR diphthong. Today, NEAR words are typically heard with a tense vowel followed by schwa (which can be seen as disyllabic), or as a long monophthong. The most frequently-occurring of these words, such as *year*, are pronounced very widely with the long monophthong. See also *here, idea* and Chap. 13.

you'll

Newer: /jɔːl/ **jɔːl**

Older: /juːl/

In RP, the preferred pronunciation of this contraction had the back GOOSE vowel, /uː/. The GOOSE vowel is now generally central, except that it's backed before a dark /l/, as in *you'll*. For many younger speakers, this back vowel is merged with the modern THOUGHT vowel [oː]. See also *cool, pool, school* and Chap. 6.

your, you're

Newer: /jɔː/ **jɔː**

Older: /jʊə/

The older pronunciation of *your* with /ʊə/ was already overtaken during the RP era by a version with the THOUGHT-NORTH vowel, making it a rhyme with *four*. /jʊə/ persisted longer as a pronunciation of *you're*, but today that word too is mostly pronounced with THOUGHT-NORTH. See also *during, poor, sure, tourist*, and Chap. 13. The quality of the modern THOUGHT-NORTH vowel is closer than in RP; see Chaps. 4 and 7.

YouTube

See *tube.*

Vowel Chart

short-lax		linking-r vowels			diphthongs (free)					
					long-tense					
KIT	ɪ	NEAR	ɪː	ɪə	FLEECE	ɪj	iː			
DRESS	ɛ	e	SQUARE	ɛː	eə	FACE	ɛj	eɪ		
LOT	ɔ	ɒ	THOUGHT	oː	ɔː	CHOICE	oj	ɔɪ		
TRAP	a	æ	PALM	ɑː		PRICE	ɑj	aɪ	MOUTH	aw	aʊ
FOOT	ɵ	ʊ	(CURE	ɵː	ʊə)				GOOSE	ʉw	uː
STRUT	ʌ		NURSE	əː	ɜː				GOAT	əw	əʊ
	comma	ə								

A phonetically and phonologically coherent chart of vowel symbols for modern SSB, with the established RP symbols in fainter text where different. The RP system has two major flaws. Firstly, it does not reflect the anti-clockwise vowel shift which has taken place (see Chap. 4). Secondly, it categorizes the vowels wrongly: its 'long monophthongs' and 'diphthongs' were not natural classes even in RP, and subsequent vowel changes have reinforced the groupings shown in this chart (see Chap. 13).

References

Carley, P., I. Mees & B. Collins (2017) *English Phonetics and Pronunciation Practice*. Routledge.

Cruttenden, A. (2014) *Gimson's Pronunciation of English*, 8th Edition. Routledge.

Ellis, A. (1869) *On Early English Pronunciation*. Trübner.

Gimson, A. C. (1962) *An Introduction to the Pronunciation of English*. Edward Arnold.

Gimson, A. C. (1977) *English Pronouncing Dictionary*, originally compiled by Daniel Jones. 14th Edition. Dent.

Gimson, A. C. (1981) 'Pronunciation in EFL dictionaries'. *Applied Linguistics* 2: 250–62.

Jones, D. (1917) *English Pronouncing Dictionary*. Dent.

Jones, D. (1918) *An Outline of English Phonetics*. Teubner.

O'Connor, J. D. & G. Arnold (1973) *Intonation of Colloquial English*, 2nd Edition. Longman.

Roach, P., J. Setter & J. Esling (2011) *The Cambridge English Pronouncing Dictionary*, 18th Edition. Cambridge University Press.

Sweet, H. (1890) *A Primer of Spoken English*. Clarendon Press.

Trudgill, P. (2000) *Sociolinguistics: An Introduction to Language and Society*, 4th Edition. Penguin.

Upton, C. & W. A. Kretzschmar Jr. (2017) *The Routledge Dictionary of Pronunciation for Current English*, 2nd Edition. Routledge.

Wells, J.C. (1982) *Accents of English*. Cambridge University Press.
Wells, J.C. (2008) *Longman Pronunciation Dictionary*, 3rd Edition. Longman.

Many articles on contemporary English phonetics and pronunciation can be found at my website, https://www.englishspeechservices.com/blog, https://www.englishspeechservices.com/words-of-the-week

Index

A

accentuation, 97
affrication, ix, 55–57
alternating stress, *see* stress
American pronunciation, x, 1, 2–4,
 11–12, 20, 29, 39, 41, 42,
 49, 56, 62, 69, 71, 73, 80,
 83–84, 93, 96, 104, 108,
 111–118, 120–121,
 124–127, 129–138,
 140–144
anti-clockwise vowel shift, 17–21,
 45, 146
apical articulation, 62
Arnold, G. F., 98–100, 103–107
aspiration, 13, 55–56
Australian pronunciation, x, 108

B

BATH vowel, 41–43
Beatles, the, 3

Bond, James, 95
British Broadcasting Corporation
 (BBC), 3, 42, 88, 101
British Empire, 2, 5

C

*Cambridge English Pronouncing
 Dictionary, see English
 Pronouncing Dictionary*
centring diphthongs, *see* diphthongs
CHOICE vowel, 24, 31, 146
closing diphthongs, *see* diphthongs
clusters, *see* consonant clusters
connected speech, 87–96
consonant clusters, viii, 56, 59–62,
 118–119, 127, 139,
 142–143
continuation patterns (intonation),
 105–106
contour, *see* intonation contour
creaky voice, *see* vocal fry

CURE vowel, viii, 18–21, 27–28, 36, 47–48, 88, 119, 135, 140–141, 146
CUrrent British English (CUBE) dictionary, x

D
dark /l/, ix, 21, 27, 28, 30, 46, 72, 115, 132, 135, 138, 144–145
diphthongs
centring diphthongs, 32, 36, 46–51, 117, 119, 126–127, 129, 135, 140–141, 143
closing diphthongs, 23–26, 31–33, 36–37, 46, 50, 88
diphthongal glides, 23–26, 31–33, 36–37
falling diphthongs, 23
'semi-diphthongs,' 23
See also vowel categories
downstep (intonation), 98–101, 103–106
DRESS vowel, 18, 19, 48, 111–112, 116–117, 120–121, 128, 130, 132, 136, 138, 140, 144, 146

E
ejectives, 14, 56–57
Ellis, Alexander, 1
English Pronouncing Dictionary, ix, 2, 47, 60, 125–126
epenthesis, 63–64, 136

F
FACE vowel, 18, 19, 24, 31, 40, 111–112, 116, 122, 124, 126, 129, 132, 134–135, 138, 143, 146
falling diphthongs, see diphthongs
Falling Head, see head (intonation)
falling intonation, 95, 96, 99–101
Fall-Rise, see nuclear tone
FLEECE vowel, ix, 18, 19, 23–26, 31, 32, 40, 49, 50, 117, 120, 125, 129, 132, 134, 137, 141, 143, 146
FOOT vowel, 18, 20, 21, 26–28, 35–37, 39, 113, 119, 124, 130, 134, 139, 141, 146
FOOT backing, 27–28
FORCE vowel, 20, 47–48
See also THOUGHT-NORTH vowel

G
G-dropping, 73–74
'General British,' 4
Gimson, A. C., vii, ix, 3, 17–21, 45, 50
glides, see diphthongal glides
glottal stop, 14, 50, 57, 67–69, 88, 91–93, 96, 141
GOAT vowel, 18, 20–21, 24, 27–30, 36, 132, 136, 144, 146
GOAT allophony, 27–28, 30
GOAT backing, 27–28, 30
GOOSE vowel, 18, 20–21, 23–28, 36, 48, 50, 113, 115, 124, 130, 134, 137–139, 141, 144–146

GOOSE backing, 27–28
GOOSE fronting, 27

H

'happY vowel,' 13, 31–33, 40, 125
hard attack, 14, 91–93
H-dropping, 73–74
head (intonation)
    Falling Head, 100
    High Head, 99, 106
    Rising Head, 101
High Bounce, *see* intonation contour
High Drop, *see* intonation contour
High Fall, *see* nuclear tone
High Head, *see* head (intonation)
High Rise, *see* nuclear tone
High Rising Terminal, *see* Uptalk

I

International Phonetic Alphabet
    (IPA), 17, 27, 29, 30, 37
    See also phonetic symbols
intonation, 14, 92, 95–108
intonation contour
    High Bounce, 107
    High Drop, 99, 100
    Low Bounce, 98, 103–105
    Low Drop, 98–100
    Terrace, 98, 106
'intrusive r,' *see* linking /r/

J

Jones, Daniel, 2, 4, 20, 21

K

KIT vowel, ix, 10, 19, 21, 26, 31–33,
    39–40, 66, 111, 116–118,
    121–123, 125–129,
    131–132, 134, 137–138,
    140–141, 144, 146

L

laminal articulation, 62
learners of English, 19, 20, 25, 37,
    39–42, 48, 56, 59, 64, 69,
    72, 74, 76, 87, 92–93,
    96–98, 100, 101, 104, 119,
    126
    See also non-native speakers
linking /r/, 24, 25, 46, 50, 87–89,
    93, 119
    'intrusive r,' 87, 119
literacy, *see* spelling
Longman Pronunciation Dictionary,
    91, 110, 126
long monophthongs, *see* vowel
    categories
long vowels, *see* vowel categories
LOT vowel, viii, 11, 18–20, 28–30,
    111–113, 121–122,
    124–125, 129, 132–134,
    137–138, 144, 146
Low Bounce, *see* intonation contour
Low Drop, *see* intonation contour
Low Fall, *see* nuclear tone
Low Rise, *see* nuclear tone
/l/ vocalization, 28, 71–72, 112,
    114, 121, 125, 132, 138,
    144

M

Mid-Level, *see* nuclear tone
monophthongization, 19, 47–51,
    143
MOUTH vowel, 21, 24, 36, 45–46,
    146
Multicultural London English
    (MLE), 46, 74
My Fair Lady, 2

N

natural class, *see* vowel categories
NEAR vowel, 21, 49, 88, 117,
    126–127, 145, 146
non-native speakers, viii, 24, 25, 56,
    75, 88, 108
    See also learners of English
NORTH vowel, *see* THOUGHT-
    NORTH vowel
nuclear tone, 97–101, 103–107
    Fall-Rise, 12, 14, 104–106
        stylized Fall-Rise, 106
    High Fall, 99–101, 106
    High Rise, 14, 104, 107–108
    Low Fall, 99–101
    Low Rise, 103–106
    Mid-Level, 105–106
NURSE vowel, 21, 88, 145, 146

O

O'Connor, J. D., 98–100, 103–107

P

PALM-START vowel, 18, 20,
    41–42, 88–89, 113, 124,
    133, 146

phonetic symbols, vii–x, 17–21, 23–25,
    27, 29–30, 32, 36–37,
    45–51, 56, 62, 109, 146
phonetic transcription, *see* phonetic
    symbols
phrasing, 24, 32, 36, 57, 68, 92, 96,
    97, 99, 100, 106
pitch-accent, *see* nuclear tone
plosive epenthesis, *see* epenthesis
pre-l breaking, 24, 50, 137
pre-fortis clipping, 24, 50
PRICE vowel, 10, 18, 19, 24, 31,
    45–46, 118, 121, 122, 146
public schools, 2, 4
    Public School Pronunciation, 2
Pygmalion, 2

R

rhoticity, 11, 71
Rising Head, *see* head (intonation)
*Routledge Dictionary of Pronunciation
    for Current English*, 19, 48

S

schwa /ə/, 13, 19, 21, 27, 30, 32,
    33, 36, 37, 39–40, 46, 48,
    50, 66, 81, 88, 92–93, 111,
    116–118, 120–138,
    140–141, 143–146
Shaw, George Bernard, 2
smoothing, 24, 46, 48–50, 118,
    126–127, 133, 143
spelling, 9–10, 13, 39–40, 56, 61,
    62, 66, 73–74, 87–88, 109,
    112, 113, 119, 121–123,
    125–126, 129–132, 135
    spelling pronunciation, 9

SQUARE vowel, ix, 18, 19, 48–49, 88, 129, 143, 146
Standard Southern British (SSB), 4
START vowel, *see* PALM-START vowel
strengthening, 11, 13–14, 56, 80, 121
stress, 11, 14, 24, 40, 55–56, 59–60, 64, 68, 73–74, 79–81, 83–84, 92, 97, 111, 114–119, 121–123, 125, 127, 129–130, 132, 135–137, 139–144
   alternating stress, 79–81
STRUT vowel, 18–20, 35, 132, 146
stylized Fall-Rise, *see* nuclear tone
Sweet, Henry, 20, 23–24, 50
syllabic consonants, 13, 65–66, 121, 127–128, 132
symbols, *see* phonetic symbols

T

Terrace, *see* intonation contour
TH-fronting, 12, 75–76, 133
THOUGHT-NORTH vowel, 18–20, 28–30, 47–48, 88–89, 112–113, 115, 119, 121, 124, 135, 137–138, 140–141, 145, 146
tonality, *see* phrasing

tone, *see* nuclear tone
tone group, *see* intonation contour
tonicity, *see* accentuation
transcription, *see* phonetic symbols
TRAP vowel, 18, 19, 41–43, 113, 122, 124, 134, 146
Trudgill, Peter, 3
/t/ voicing, 11, 69

U

Uptalk, 11, 104, 107–108

V

vocal fry, 11, 95–96
vowel categories, 25, 49–51, 146

W

weak vowel merger, 11, 33, 39–40
Wells, John, x, 4, 59, 91, 110
writing, *see* spelling

Y

yes-no questions, 14, 103–105, 107
yod coalescence, 11, 59–60
YouGlish, x, 110
YouTube, x, 142, 145